The TUTANKHAMUN DECEPTION

The True Story
of the
Mummy's Curse

GERALD O'FARRELL

PAN BOOKS

First published 2001 by Sidgwick & Jackson

This edition published 2002 by Pan Books
an imprint of Pan Macmillan Ltd
Pan Macmillan, 20 New Wharf Road, London N1 9RR
Basingstoke and Oxford
Associated companies throughout the world
www.panmacmillan.com

ISBN 0 330 44490 5

3 5 7 9 8 6 4 2

A CIP catalogue record for this book is available from
the British Library.

Typeset by SetSystems Ltd, Saffron Walden, Essex
Printed and bound in Great Britain by
Mackays of Chatham plc, Chatham, Kent

This book is dedicated to Charles Pope.
His brilliant work will illuminate the biblical darkness,
a work which Ahmed started so many years ago.
I am honoured to call both of them my friends.
Their investigative research will allow
our children's children to finally begin
the long journey back to the stars.

CONTENTS

Contents

ACKNOWLEDGEMENTS

First and foremost, I wish to thank my partner, Sheena MacBrayne, for her help and perseverance over the past several years. My sister Pauline Jendro for the countless hours at the computer and my dear friend Fiona Spencer Thomas, my literary agent, who had such great faith in me and my project. Also Andrew Crofts for the countless hours spent in rearranging my manuscript.

There are many in Egypt that I would like to express my thanks to but cannot by name, so I will just say 'thanks to my friends the Inspectors of Antiquities' and they will know that I haven't forgotten them.

My deep and heartfelt thanks to my friend Ahmed Osman who has taught me so much and given so much new understanding to the world on biblical history. For help and support, Richard Craske, Angela and Andrew, Beverley Milne-Browne and her mother Lin, Ian McLeod and to Stuart Seemark and Jo. To my friends at Macmillan, a humble thanks for all they have done, especially Gordon Wise and Ingrid Connell.

In the US Tony and Beth-Ann, Peg and Randy and my old friend Armin. Many thanks Thomas Hoving for opening my eyes.

Gerald O'Farrell

Map of Egypt

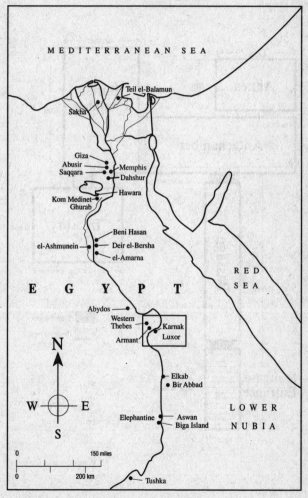

MEDITERRANEAN SEA

Teil el-Balamun

Sakha

Giza
Abusir
Saqqara
Memphis
Dahshur

Kom Medinet
Ghurab
Hawara

Beni Hasan
el-Ashmunein
Deir el-Bersha
el-Amarna

E G Y P T

RED
SEA

Abydos
Western
Thebes
Karnak
Armant
Luxor

Elkab
Bir Abbad

N

W E

S

Elephantine
Aswan
Biga Island

LOWER

NUBIA

0   150 miles

0   200 km

Tushka

Plan of Tutankhamun's Tomb

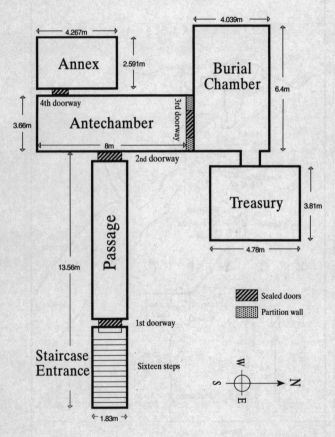

The Valley of the Kings

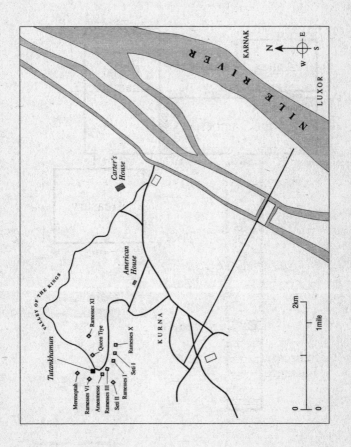

INTRODUCTION

Tutankhamun and the discovery of his tomb was the greatest show on earth in the 1920s and remained so for decades afterwards. The whole world heard about it and was desperate to know more. Egyptology, which had previously been the preserve of an elite few, was suddenly transformed into an international soap opera with one cliffhanger after another. The revelation of the story of the boy pharaoh, with its seductive mixture of intrigue, wealth, mystery and royalty, opened the eyes of the general public to an ancient civilization, and whetted their appetite to find out more. It was to prove a lasting fascination.

What the readers of the newspapers at the time didn't know was that the discovery of the tomb was actually one of the most daring hoaxes in history, devised by two Englishmen of repute to cover up what was probably the greatest robbery of precious jewels and gold bullion there has ever been or is ever likely to be. The two men, Howard Carter and Lord Carnarvon, were hailed as heroes at the time of the discovery, but in this book are revealed to have had feet of clay. They were, in fact, showmen and dissemblers of breathtaking skill and audacity.

Many of the scholars and experts who have written about the discovery over the years have hinted that things might not have been quite as Carter and Carnarvon described them but, until now, no one has actually managed to work out the full extent of their crime. For nearly a century the world has believed a story which is almost entirely fictitious and which enabled Carter and Carnarvon to secretly enrich themselves and their associates beyond anyone's wildest dreams of avarice.

They manipulated the media and the politicians of the world with an adroitness that would be the envy of any modern press baron or spin doctor, but, in the course of their robbery, which took them nearly ten years to pull off, they uncovered a secret so potentially explosive that even they didn't know how to exploit it. By suppressing the truth they changed the course of history, perhaps costing millions of people their lives, and in the end they were almost certainly murdered for what they knew, along with a number of others.

Stories of tomb raiders and 'mummy's curses' have become part of international folklore since that fateful discovery in 1922, but none of them is as extraordinary or dramatic as the true story of what went on in those ancient tombs and passageways beneath the desert sands. In this book I tell the story of how I believe Carter and Carnarvon got away with this fantastic heist and how their discoveries, if they were ever fully revealed, would change the way the whole world thinks. The official version of what happened is one of the most exciting and romantic stories in history; the true version is even more extraordinary.

My fascination with Egypt began when my second wife and I took a trip to Cairo in 1970. Standing on the Giza plateau, in the shadow of the Great Pyramid of Cheops, I determined to find out just how it had been built, by whom and why. It became an obsession. I read all I could find and returned there as often as time and finances permitted. It ultimately became obvious to me that the great god genius, Imhotep, had not only designed and built the Step Pyramid at Saqqara for King Zoser, but also the pyramids on the Giza plateau for the pharaohs Cheops (Khufu), Chephren and Mycerenus. The thinking at the time was that there was a gap of two or three hundred years between these constructions, but this gap has since been shortened to today's estimate of seventy-five years.

Imhotep was the first man to emerge from the mists of history as a flesh and blood creature. As he exercised my thinking, so also did another figure who was to loom large on Egypt's stage much later, the pharaoh Akhenaten. More than fifteen hundred years separated these two great men and yet, for me, they were inextricably linked. I could not write about Imhotep without thinking of Akhenaten (the pharaoh generally thought to have been Tutankhamun's father), and the Eighteenth Dynasty.

As previously I had been led to Cairo, I found myself, in 1994, drawn to Luxor, to the Valley of the Kings and to the tomb of Tutankhamun. Once again I was puzzled as to why I should be attracted with such intensity to a simple tomb in the valley where a young boy king had been buried with his vast treasures so long ago. I would stand fascinated, gazing at the enigmatic figure lying in his sarcophagus in that bare, gloomy burial chamber, the only discovered pharaoh who remains in his tomb today. Or was it his tomb? The oddest thoughts crowded in on me as I pondered that perhaps this was not so. Perhaps nothing here was quite as it appeared. The idea seemed so preposterous that I pushed it to the back of my mind; but it would not go away and it was only after I read Thomas Hoving's masterly work, *Tutankhamun: The Untold Story*, that I knew I was not mad, that it was possible the accepted version of events was wrong, and I set out to find the facts.

Hoving is a former head of New York's Metropolitan Museum of Art, an organization which was intimately involved in the discovery and clearance of the tomb and holds many of the treasures. He stated clearly that he did not accept the official story which was put forward at the time, but I felt there was still more which he had not yet uncovered. Unlike the Museum of Antiquities in Cairo, which also has a bewildering amount of items removed from the tomb during the twenties and thirties, the Metropolitan Museum in New York has a sterile clinical atmosphere: the objects on display robbed of their personality by the perfection of their surroundings. They seem as cold and remote as the museum itself, an establishment which played a crucial part in the process of denuding many of the tombs of Egypt.

The following is the story which I have pieced together after years of research in the museums, libraries and private collections of the world, and from interviews with the authors of many of the books I most admire on the subject, including Hoving. It pulls together the many different strands of this complicated story which stretches over three millennia, but concentrates on the early years of the twentieth century up to the death of Sigmund Freud, whose controversial theories on the subject of Egyptology, I believe, led to a plot being hatched for his murder.

1

THE GREATEST TREASURE
HUNT ON EARTH

May your spirit live, may you spend millions of years,
you who love Thebes, sitting with your face to the north wind,
your eyes beholding happiness . . . "[1]
Inscription on the Wishing Cup from the tomb of Tutankhamun

On the surface the Valley of the Kings is the same beautiful
hell-hole today as it was at the beginning of the twentieth century.
It is not so very different to how this valley was three thousand
years ago, or even thirty thousand. A timeless place of infinite
fascination, filled with secrets and mysteries and hideous discom-
forts for those mortals who choose to spend their working lives
there.

It lies about six hundred kilometres south of Cairo, the present-
day capital of Egypt, near the Nile. Across the river is the city of
Luxor, once called Thebes and one of the greatest capitals of the
ancient world. This dusty, dried-up river valley is the most magnificent burial ground in the world. During the second millennium BC,
Egyptian workers quarried a series of tombs beneath this valley,
decorating them with mysterious predictions of the underworld and
filling them with treasures. There, with infinite care and artistry,
they laid out the mummified and bejewelled bodies of their rulers

5

and surrounded them with their belongings, making the valley one of the greatest sacred sites in history.

'The very name is full of romance,' Thomas Hoving writes in *Tutankhamun: The Untold Story*. 'But one cannot imagine a more remote, unpleasant, hot, dried-out, lonely place anywhere in the world. In this valley head, far from every sound of life, once lay buried, in their sleep of a million years times infinity, thirty of the greatest kings ancient Egypt had known.'[2]

There are some eighty-five known tombs in the Valley of the Kings. Twenty-five of these being the tombs of the pharaohs of the New Kingdom period, that is, the period between about 1550 BC to 1319 BC, and include some of the great rulers of the ancient world, Tuthmosis III, Ramesses II and, of course, Tutankhamun (1333–1323 BC). The tombs range from simple pits with rectangular burial chambers to tombs with corridors, rooms and grand burial chambers. Many of these survive and some are among the finest sculptured and painted monuments of ancient Egypt.[3]

During the New Kingdom, Egypt exercised her greatest power and for nearly five hundred years the city of Thebes, on the eastern bank of the Nile, was the country's spiritual capital. In millennia gone by, its influence and notoriety spread throughout the known world. In Homer's famous work it was referred to as 'the fabled city of a hundred gates'[4] and, as such, the Greeks named it Thebes after their own great city, while the Egyptians called it 'Waset' meaning 'dominion'.[5] Now it is called by its Arabic name, Luxor. Eventually, the capital of Egypt moved away to the north, and for five hundred years the valley remained deathly quiet until the arrival of the Greeks in the second century AD.

On the other side of the river lay the Kingdom of Osiris, the 'Lord of the Afterlife'. During the Eighteenth Dynasty, it was here that the kings, for their burial, selected a brand new location. Abandoning the earlier custom of pyramid building, they opted for deep rock-cut tombs instead. Isolated and relatively easy to guard, but also close to Thebes, these inhospitable valleys were regarded as the ideal location to develop as the new royal necropolis. Even the mountains surrounding it resembled an *akhet*, the hieroglyphic symbol for horizon. Today, this windswept gorge is more commonly known by tourists as the Valley of the Kings.[6]

Eventually, the political and spiritual centre of Egypt moved away to the north and for five hundred years after the last royal burial there the valley remained relatively quiet until the Greeks arrived. They came as tourists, complete with the guide books of the time, to see the sights, some of them leaving comments scratched into walls and rocks: 'I have seen the peculiarly excellent workmanship of these tombs, which is unutterable to us.'

The first serious published work on the tombs in the valley appeared in 1743 as *Observations on Egypt*, by Englishman Richard Pococke, subsequently a bishop. In 1798 Napoleon Bonaparte landed in Egypt with his forces, bringing 139 learned scholars with him to study and chronicle the country and its history, a project which resulted in the publication of the highly regarded *Description de l'Egypte* between 1809 and 1816. The discovery of the Rosetta Stone (deciphered a few years later) provided academics with the ability to read hieroglyphic script and Egyptology became widely fashionable for the first time in Western Europe, but still only amongst the very rich and educated.

Arthur Weigall, a distinguished archaeologist active at the beginning of the twentieth century and a man who figures prominently in this story, was of the opinion that students of Egyptology would be far better served if they visited Egypt rather than having Egypt visit them through the medium of the museum. As he put it:

> The narrow-minded policy of certain European and American museums whose desire it is, at all costs, to place Egyptian and other eastern antiquities actually before the eyes of western students in order that they may have the comfort and entertainment of examining, at home, the wonders of the lands which they make no effort to visit. I have no hesitation in saying that the craze for recklessly dragging away unique monuments from Egypt to be exhibited in western museums for the satisfaction of the untravelled man is the most pernicious bit of folly to be found in the whole broad realm of Egyptological misbehaviour.[7]

Arthur Weigall wasn't the only one appalled by the way in which explorers worked. The renowned nineteenth-century English traveller and translator of the *Arabian Nights*, Sir Richard Burton, wrote, 'Nile-land was then, as now, a field for plunder; fortunes were made by digging, not gold, but antiques; and the archaeological field became a battle plain for two armies of Dragomans and Fellah-navvies.'[8]

In 1877, in *Egypt As It Is*, explorer J. C. McCoan wrote, 'Shipment of bones high on Egypt's export list. They contribute nearly as much as those of modern cattle to a yearly total of ten thousand tons . . .'[9]

And as Sir Frederick Henniker said, '. . . those buildings that have withstood the attacks of Barbarians, will not resist the speculation of civilised cupidity, virtuosi, and antiquarians.'[10]

Giovanni Battista Belzoni, an Italian engineer who had at one time earned a living as a circus strongman under the name the 'Patagonian Sampson', arrived in Egypt in 1815, trying to sell a water-lifting device. Failing to make any money that way, he was hired by Henry Salt, the English Consul-General, to transport the giant head of Ramesses II to the Nile for shipment back to London. His success working for Salt led Belzoni to explore further and he succeeded in discovering a number of important tombs, including those of Ramesses I and Sethos I. Belzoni became famous and many others followed in his footsteps.

Unlike so many of the most awesome natural and historical sights of the world, urban development has not encroached on the Valley of the Kings, despite the enormous curiosity which the world has felt for it. Thebes may have become the modern city of Luxor, but it has still not crept across the river and plain towards this sacred place; the valley is still one of the hottest, bleakest and most silent places on earth, the stark scenery dwarfing the small clusters of temporary stalls which spring up each morning, selling trinkets and postcards to tourists who want to prove that they have actually been to this mythical place. The vegetation on the western bank, fed by the waters of the Nile, ends abruptly at more or less the same place now as it did when the archaeologists who were to make the most famous discoveries first set foot there. There is still only one entrance to the valley, which was what made it easy to guard, and no exit unless you are willing to scale the rocks of the sheer cliffs which rise all around, baked to alternating pink and gold by the relentless glare of the sun.

When you arrive it is hard to imagine that this is the place where the Thebans built tombs similar to those in other parts of Egypt but on a monumental scale not seen elsewhere. Beneath the hot shifting dust and sand lie the intended final resting places of their greatest pharaohs, all but invisible from the surface but vividly engraved in all our imaginations. So far, Egyptologists have discovered over eighty tombs and pits in the area; no one knows how many more there may be as yet undiscovered or destined to remain silent and undisturbed for all eternity. Nor does anyone know what treasures may still lie in these hidden tombs; and that is what draws most of us. Every child is intrigued by hidden treasure and it is an idea that never leaves us, even when we grow to adulthood.

With the passing years childhood tales of pirate treasure buried on desert islands give way to more grown-up fantasies. Some people dive to the floors of oceans in search of wrecked ships and their precious cargoes, while others spend all their leisure hours walking back and forth across the landscape with metal detectors, head-phones clamped to their ears, their faces closed in concentration as they stare at the ground, willing it to yield up some previously missed ancient coin or similar treasure.

Some spend years panning for nuggets of gold amidst miles of mud, while others dive for pearls in beds of oysters or fossick for opals in the Australian Outback. Hunters of easy fortunes have drilled all over the surface of the earth in search of oil and scoured endless attics in the hope of discovering lost masterpieces of the art world. For those of us who want the thrill of the hunt without any of the effort there is always the lottery ticket bought in the hope that it will reveal where fate has hidden the prize money. None of us is completely free of these dreams.

But the buried treasure of the pharaohs is the greatest prize of all because it is reserved only for those brave enough to tolerate the hardships of the desert and clever enough to know what they are looking for. It is both a physical and intellectual challenge, and therefore promises double the rewards to those who succeed.

It has always been widely known that the pharaohs were buried with all their worldly wealth beside them to assure them a comfortable eternity in the afterlife, and the contents of a tomb are often described. To start with there would be the mummified body of the pharaoh himself, which would wear a face mask showing how he looked when alive, while the body would be decorated with gold and jewels. The mummy would be in a series of coffins carved in his own shape, which nested inside one another and were gilded, or perhaps even made of solid gold. The largest of the coffins would be inside a stone sarcophagus with a heavy carved lid, which would itself be contained within a series of gilded wooden shrines.

All around the shrines, and sometimes in adjoining rooms, would be stored the items which the dead ruler would need to sustain him on his travels through the underworld, to demonstrate his importance in this world and to show that he should be accorded similar honours on the other side. There would also be life-sized, gilded figures and models of guards and field workers, and many smaller statuettes. There would be chariots and boats to transport the pharaoh through the afterlife, and intricately carved couches, along with everyday objects like clothing, furniture, musical instruments, games, perfumes and cosmetics, baskets, boxes and chests, lamps and writing materials, weapons, tableware, food and anything else which he might possibly need for his sojourn in eternity. During the mummification process the internal organs of the pharaoh would be removed and embalmed and sealed into canopic jars which would also be stored in the tomb.

Preparations for a pharoah's death would begin many years before he actually died and sometimes objects from one tomb were reused by a later king, a practice which muddies the waters for the archaeologists as they attempt to unravel the mysteries of each tomb and its occupant. The location of the tomb would normally be decided as soon as the king ascended to his throne and he, with his priests, would oversee the design, building and decoration of the rooms during his reign. The actual work would be done by villagers from Deir el-Medina on the other side of the mountains. Each day an army of architects, quarrymen, plasterers, draughtsmen, sculptors and decorators would arrive at dawn and labour for eight hours to create these works of art.

Imagination has elaborated these established facts and the more gullible have come to believe that prodigious quantities of gold and jewellery are simply waiting, preserved in massive tombs, for the smartest and most intrepid among us to uncover. There was a time when such fantasies were rooted in reality, but with each new discovery the chances that it will be the last increase. And, as with all myths of easy pickings, nothing is ever as simple as it seems. In any gold rush most of the dreamers end up finding a few small prizes which they quickly squander in the euphoria of the moment. Just as nature hides her mineral riches and precious metals, the ancient Egyptians worked hard to make sure that their treasures were well buried; those that were not have long since been plundered in the three thousand years or so since the tombs were built.

Moreover, there has always been plenty of competition: at the beginning of the twentieth century everyone wanted a piece of whatever treasure might still be beneath the desert, including bandits in search of a quick profit and governments who wanted to protect assets which they believed should belong to the people or posterity, or perhaps to themselves. At this point in history when

Western Europeans, particularly the British, bestrode the world, adventure in dangerous foreign lands was what all hot-blooded young men dreamed of, particularly those with the money and position to travel in style. Just as they went to Africa and India to shoot big game, a few of the most adventurous sailed to Egypt to search for buried treasure.

Egypt was a destination which appealed to the more educated travellers; as well as the possibility of unlimited gold, it also offered the intellectual stimulation of uncovering the past in an area steeped in more history than any other. The baser aspects of treasure hunting could be justified by the higher aims of archaeological study. But the upper-class travellers from wealthier countries were not the only people searching for treasure. There were also the people from villages in the surrounding areas who had been living off the proceeds of what they could find for generations. For them it was as natural as it was for an African tribesman to hunt antelope in order to sell the skins, or elephants for their ivory. Just as a farmer in Texas might now drill for oil on his land, these people searched continually for whatever might have been secreted by the ancients, sometimes finding stray objects sent to the surface by movements of the earth or sudden floods, and occasionally stumbling across new hoards hidden in the network of tombs to which they had managed to gain access. The desecration of the tombs had been going on for thousands of years. Men burrowed in the earth like moles for anything that shone or glittered in the harsh sunlight. Gold, in whatever form, was the prize most eagerly sought, or jewellery that could be either sold intact or broken up. The bodies of the kings were of no interest to the thieves except where there was the possibility of jewellery on the mummified remains. Mummified bodies were torn apart in the frantic search for anything of value. It should be pointed out here that although these depredations had been going on through the millennia, by far the greatest proportion took place after the original Egyptians had been conquered or had died out.

These local people, whose ancestors had been living off the land for generations, were the true experts. They might not have known the provenance or historical significance of the objects they found, but they knew their value on the local market. Some items would find their way from the local stalls to the grander antique shops catering to tourists and exporters, others would be traded surreptitiously in a backstreet somewhere, produced from the folds of a cloak with a hissed sales pitch.

When the English gentlemen arrived in Egypt from Victorian and Edwardian Britain, or their French counterparts and the newly rich American leisured classes, they were by no means the first visitors to come searching for booty. Europeans had been coming to Egypt and the Valley of the Kings for two hundred years by then, the scholars gradually unravelling the history of the area and marvelling at the art while removing whatever artefacts they could obtain to their own countries. However, despite all this activity, Egyptology was still a primitive discipline, amateurish in many respects. What little knowledge there was of pharaonic Egypt was confused, and still is. The time of the pharaohs was known as the 'mystical era' with as many differing views of the truth as there have been writers to advance them. In his book, *The Lost Pharaohs*, Leonard Cottrell wrote, 'Finally, as a dreadful warning to any other amateur Egyptologist who is tempted to sail these perilous seas, here are some of the scholastic cross-currents he will have to encounter . . .'[11] And he proceeded to list some of the many contradictory statements that have been made down the years by the 'experts'. The archaeologists who arrived from Europe may have believed themselves to come from a more civilized part of the world, but they did as much damage to the treasures they were seeking as the local thieves and the more sensitive among them were horrified by what they saw happening.

In her book, *A Thousand Years up the Nile*, published in 1877, Amelia Edwards, founder of the Egyptian Exploration Society, expressed her regrets at the way in which the work had been conducted. 'We soon became hardened to such sights,' she wrote, 'and learned to rummage among dusty sepulchres with no more compunction than would have befitted a gang of body snatchers. These are the experiences upon which one looks back afterwards with wonder and something like remorse; but so infectious is the universal callousness and so over-mastering is the passion for relic hunting that I do not doubt we should again do the same thing under the same circumstances.'[12]

The distinguished archaeologist, Sir Flinders Petrie, was equally appalled. In his autobiography, *Seventy Years of Archaeology*, he wrote of one French archaeologist working the royal tomb of Abydos who, 'kept no plans, and boasted that he burnt up the remains of the woodwork of the First Dynasty in his kitchen'.[13] Petrie complained that the man's finds were scattered amongst his financial partners in Paris and sold by auction. 'Nothing seems to be done with any uniform or regular plan,' Petrie lamented. 'Work is begun and left unfinished, no regard is paid to future requirements of explorations; and no civilised or labour-saving appliances are used, nothing but what the natives have; all the sand being carried in small baskets on the heads of children. It is sickening to see the rate at which everything is being destroyed, and the little regard paid to its preservation ... anything would be better than leaving things to be destroyed wholesale; better spoil half in preserving the other half, than leave the whole to be smashed...'[14] Later he wrote, 'The science of observation of registration of recording was as yet unthought of; nothing had a meaning unless it were an inscription or a sculpture. A year's work in Egypt made me feel it was like a house on fire, so rapid was the destruction going on, my duty was that of a salvage man, to get all I could quickly gather in and then, when I was sixty, I would sit down and write it up. That was the true forecast.'[15]

If it was confusing for those who had studied it, Egyptology was even more baffling for the general public, who showed little interest in the discoveries of their betters until 1923, when everything would change with the emergence from his peaceful rest beneath the earth into the glare of twentieth-century publicity, after almost three thousand years of peace and obscurity, of one of the most famous historical figures of all time.

Today, if you visit the tomb of Tutankhamun you find yourself in a small underground room beneath a barren hillside with the sad battered body of the young king stripped of all his once colossal worldly goods. Visitors to the tomb can often be heard complaining at how little there is to see for the money they have been charged at the door, just the three-thousand-year-old remains of a boy they know nothing about, with only one of the bewitching golden masks that have become so famous remaining. But that is what is so extraordinary about the experience.

This boy was actually one of the most special people in history, possibly even *the* most special, the story of his short life having shaped everything about the world we all live in. And yet he has been abandoned for us all to troop past and stare at and be disappointed by. Where is the mystical show of power and wealth that we have all heard about? How can such a momentous story have originated in such a small, cramped set of rooms?

About six hundred kilometres away in the Cairo Museum it's a different story. There the visitor's breath is taken away by the wonders on show, wonders that just eighty years ago were lying around the lonely boy in the tomb, protecting him from the vicissitudes of the next life. Now they stand, displayed in a glory of light and glass far removed from the airless blackness of the tomb where they lay unseen and unadmired for the better part of three thousand years.

The beauty and richness of what was discovered in that tomb is hard to comprehend without looking at it with your own eyes. The amount of gold is dazzling, but it is also the elegance of the craftsmanship which leaves the viewer breathless. These are items created by the greatest craftsmen then working, for kings who were seen as gods. They are acts of worship as well as demonstrations of worldly importance. Every artefact and every piece of furniture has been lovingly carved and gilded, and many inlaid with meticulous care and attention. It is a demonstration of wealth and power which has seldom been equalled in history and never preserved so well.

In at least a dozen other museums around the world there are similar displays of contents from the tomb, each one an extravaganza of craftsmanship, wealth and beauty. If they were all put together the effect would be overwhelming, and we are told that this is less than half of what the boy was actually buried with when he died; approximately 60 per cent was taken by robbers. The thought must strike anyone who sees this display that this boy was somebody quite extraordinary, somebody greater than we have so far been led to believe.

When the contents of the Cairo exhibition went on the road in the 1970s, touring major European capitals, millions of people queued to join the crowds that inched past, shoulder to shoulder, to marvel at the extraordinary displays. It was the greatest, richest archaeological rock-and-roll tour of all time. Nothing like it has ever happened before or since. The name of Tutankhamun was on everyone's lips and the impassive gold coffin carvings and death mask became not only one of the most lasting, but also one of the most familiar images in the world, staring out from newspapers, magazines, posters and television sets three thousand years after the boy died.

But who exactly was he? And how did he come from virtual anonymity to become overnight one of the most famous names of ancient history?

2

THE SIGNIFICANCE
OF TUTANKHAMUN

The mystery of his life still eludes us – the shadows move
but the dark is never quite dispersed.[1]
Howard Carter

At the time of his discovery by Howard Carter in 1922, no one knew much about Tutankhamun, or was even that interested. It was hardly a name that stuck in the memory of schoolchildren or their teachers, not like King Arthur, William the Conqueror, Alexander the Great or Attila the Hun.

To those learned few who did know the name, he was one of the most insignificant of the pharaohs, mainly because he reigned for such a short time – probably only about ten years – and died at the age of eighteen or nineteen, partly because his tomb was so well hidden, and also because his successors had made sure his name was erased from history along with that of his family. It was generally believed that he was little more than a figurehead: a young boy who inherited a title but saw his kingdom ruled by a regent for most of his life. It was also thought he was probably murdered, but nobody, apart from the most avid of scholars, was too interested either way. As Howard Carter, the man who will prove central to our story, once said, 'We might say with truth that the one outstanding feature of his life was that he died and was buried.' Not exactly promising material for the building of an international reputation as a giant figure of ancient history.[2]

In 1907 the Egyptian government, planning to reclaim a large area of the Nile Delta for agricultural purposes, decided to have the height of the Aswan Dam raised seven metres. This meant flooding a large area of the Nubian desert in what is now the Sudan approximately 250 kilometres in length and one kilometre wide on both sides of the Nile. This flooding would cover many ancient cemeteries and remains, so the Egyptian government gave the job of excavation and conservation to Sir Grafton Elliot Smith of the School of Medicine in Cairo, who made a thorough investigation of the many thousands of skeletons that were exhumed. Smith's forte was the examination of skulls and his meticulous attention to detail led him to conclude that, mixed in with the Egyptian stock (the brown race), were aliens who he described as probably belonging to the 'Armenoid race', the inhabitants of south-east Europe.

In 1912 he wrote:

The alien people present many striking features of contrast which sharply differentiate them from the population of Egypt and Nubia. In height they do not differ in any marked degree, but their crania are shorter and considerably broader than those of the indigenous people. The nose is much narrower, more prominent and high-bridged than that of the Egyptian or Nubian, and in comparison with the latter, the nasal spine is much more prominent. The orbits of the alien people are distinguished by their large size and rounded form and by the frequent occurrence of large deficiencies in the lateral walls . . . but no part of the skeleton presents such peculiarly distinctive features as the mandible. Its high ascending ramus and over-grown coronoid process enables us to distinguish the remains of an alien from an Egyptian, a Nubian or a Negro at a glance, even if no other part of the skeleton is available for examination.[5]

These people, Elliot Smith concluded, were more than intelligent enough to accomplish the amazing building feats that the modern world marvels at on the banks of the Nile, and it was the greatest among them that lay beneath the ground in the hidden tombs of the Valley of the Kings. Nobody knows just who these blue-eyed, fair-skinned people were, or even where they came from, which adds greatly to the air of mystery surrounding them and stokes the many myths which have sprung up. Anthropologically, they were termed Caucasians.[4] But the archaeologists working at the beginning of the twentieth century knew nothing of this and were much more interested in hunting out the tombs of the big names of the five-hundred-year period which encompassed the Eighteenth, Nineteenth and Twentieth Dynasties. They were inspired by names such as Akhenaten and Ramesses the Great, not Tutankhamun.

Tutankhamun was part of the extraordinary Eighteenth Dynasty, all of whose pharaohs were buried in the Valley of the Kings. In many cases their tombs, beneath those of the later Ramesside kings, had become hidden and were less accessible to early explorers. One of the reasons that so little was known about the boy king was that almost none of his treasures had found their way out of his tomb and into the antiquities market before the twentieth century. The dealers therefore had no reason to tell his story to their customers. If there was no product to sell, they didn't need to build a myth in order to create a market. But the product was there, lying in wait beneath the rocks like an historical time bomb waiting to detonate, and one or two of the most determined of the explorers were convinced of that fact.

All that was known about Tutankhamun was that he had probably succeeded to the throne after either a pharaoh called Smenkhkara, who was believed by some to be his brother, or Akhenaten, who was thought to be his father. Little was certain about Smenkhkara, but Akhenaten was known to have been a strong ruler who had caused chaos in the kingdom by forcing his people to abandon their traditional belief in a pantheon of gods in favour of a single deity, Aten, the sun god, who Akhenaten believed to be in everything. This was a radical and heretical creed for the time but one which was eventually to become the foundation of Judaism, Christianity and Islam. However, while Akhenaten worshipped just one god, all the people had to worship through him, making him a god-king.

The general belief among scholars was that whereas Akhenaten had been a strong ruler, Tutankhamun was weak.[5] But being Akhenaten's son meant that to many at the time the boy was the Son of God. 'Messiah' is a word taken from the Egyptian word for crocodile – *messer* – because kings were anointed with the grease of the crocodile, just as they anoint rulers today with sacred oil.[6] However insignificant this young pharaoh might have seemed to the explorers who came to the valley three thousand years after he died, he would certainly have been important to the people who buried him.[7] When his coffin was finally opened it was discovered that Tutankhamun had two plain straps of golden leaves lying on his breast, joined with a knot. Mere kings of every period wore these decorations with one strap, but the gods were always given two. Someone, at the time of the burial, believed that this insignificant boy was a god.

Who the boy's mother was is still a mystery today, but the most widely accepted belief was that it was Kiya, one of Akhenaten's secondary wives. She appears to have been Aknenaten's 'favourite', and was honoured in Egypt with sanctuaries and chapels of her own. In a number of reliefs she is pictured with a child but there is no certainty that this is Tutankhamun.[8]

Akhenaten and his most important wife, Nefertiti, had five principal daughters, the second eldest called Ankhesenpaaten. Although a little older than Tutankhamun it was this half-sister who became his wife. The young couple probably had two children who died in infancy, since two tiny mummified corpses were discovered in the tomb of Tutankhamun.

Since he was still a boy when he came to the throne, maybe eight or nine years of age, it seems likely that throughout Tutankhamun's reign power was probably held by a few senior officials in the royal court. One such adviser was the 'Grand Vizier' named Ay, who is believed by some historians to have been Nefertiti's father. It was probably Ay who decided who would and who wouldn't have access to the young king.

As Tutankhamun and his wife had no surviving children, upon the boy-king's death Ay duly became pharaoh. Reigning for only four years, he was followed by one of Egypt's greatest generals, Horemheb, the first pharaoh of the Nineteenth Dynasty. Upon his own accession to the throne, Horemheb immediately set out to erase all trace not only of Akhenaten's reign but also that of Smenkhkara, Tutankhamun and Ay. He outlawed the use of their names, destroyed their temples, toppled their statues, defaced their reliefs and chiselled out their inscriptions.[9] Within fifty years of Akhenaten's death, he and Tutankhamun, together with Ay, were erased from the records as if they never existed. They were removed from the history books before they had even been written.[10]

Because Tutankhamun was left out of the lists of rulers, it was not long before his name was virtually forgotten; grave robbers knew nothing about him and so did not bother to search for his tomb. It is even possible that some of the later kings were ignorant of his existence. When Ramesses VI constructed his own tomb two hundred years later he may have been unaware that he was building across the blocked-up entrance of the boy-king's burial place. The only clues to Tutankhamun's existence were occasional modest fragments inscribed with his name which Egyptologists turned up in their searchings in the desert. There was never any find significant enough to alert anyone to just what lay in store.[11]

By the beginning of the twentieth century it was generally believed that the Valley of the Kings had been exhausted, that all the treasure that was going to be found had been found. But some of the most determined adventurers and scholars, most notably an obstinate young Englishman called Howard Carter, were not yet ready to give up the hunt and still held on to the hope that they would find the tomb of this little known king and that it would tell them all that they wanted to know about the customs of the times. They had little idea what they would discover if they located Tutankhamun's tomb, they just knew that they wanted to continue searching.[12]

To many, including the Egyptian authorities, this endless quest seemed little more than quixotic bravado, as futile as searching for the Yeti in the high Himalayas or the prehistoric monster believed by some to dwell in the depths of Loch Ness. But no one can stop dreamers from dreaming and two of the boldest of dreamers, Howard Carter and the Earl of Carnarvon, were about to join forces and make history.

3

HOWARD CARTER –
LESS THAN A GENTLEMAN

*Mr Carter is a good-natured lad whose interest is entirely
in painting and natural history ... it is no use to
me to work him up as an excavator*[1]
Professor W. M. Flinders Petrie

When he first arrived in Luxor there was little about the young
middle class English boy, Howard Carter, to suggest that one day
his name would go down in history as the most spectacularly
successful of Egyptologists.

Carter was born in Putney, in London, on 9 May 1874, but spent
most of his childhood in the Norfolk town of Swaffham. His father
was an artist, making his living from painting portraits of animals
belonging to the local gentry and doing illustrations for the *Illustrated London News*. Carter was the youngest of eleven children and
his father must have had a very limited income. Since his family
could not afford to send him to school Howard was tutored at home;
he felt his lack of education keenly all his life. 'It is said,' he later
wrote, 'that nature thrusts some of us into the world miserably
incomplete.'[2]

He learnt to paint meticulously correctly from his father and was
very able at recording how an animal or a house or a village scene

might look. His work was cold, clinical and competent but had none of the flair or personality of great art. Although the Carter family were known to the local gentry for the services they provided, they were not members of that class, a fact that had a profound early effect on Howard's brooding personality. At the end of the nineteenth century the English class system was rigid and few people were able to rise from modest beginnings. There was no reason for anyone to assume that Howard would ever amount to anything.

Then fortune smiled on him. A young professor from the Egyptian Museum of Antiquities, Percy Newberry, told a friend of his, the future Lady Amherst of Hackney, while visiting her at her home in Norfolk, that he was looking for someone to help him with some drawings he was undertaking in Egypt, tracing the hieroglyphs of ancient monuments. Lady Amherst suggested the teenaged Howard Carter; the boy had done some work for her with which she had been pleased. This was a rare opportunity for a young man to improve his situation. Sometimes it was possible for people from the English middle classes to improve their social standing through a profession, perhaps by joining the church or the army or through academic or political distinction or aristocratic patronage; Carter, however, while greatly wishing to move up the social scale from his lower middle class origins, never acquired the necessary social ease or charm. He was to become an irascible loner of a man, more so with every passing year, not in the least clubbable or diplomatic. 'I have a hot temper,' he later wrote, 'and that amount of tenacity of purpose which unfriendly observers sometimes call obstinacy, and which nowadays ... it pleases my enemies to term ... *mauvaise caractère*. Well, that I can't help.'[5]

All this, however, was still some way in the future when he was first approached by Professor Newberry. He was just seventeen years old, nearly the same age as Tutankhamun had been when he died, and his only saleable skill was as a watercolourist.

Newberry offered Carter exactly the sort of opportunity that he needed and Howard accepted it gratefully, moving to London to work in the British Museum. It isn't hard to imagine how intimidating but exciting it must have been for a young boy from the provinces to start work at such an august British establishment. It would have been exciting because he was getting his first taste of the work and world that he was going to be immersing himself in for the rest of his life, intimidating because he was surrounded by highly educated men, all of them the products of famous schools and great universities.

Diligent and skilful in everything he undertook, Carter impressed Professor Newberry and was invited, after just three months at the museum, to become the most junior member of the staff of the Egyptian Exploration Fund, which was carrying out excavations in the Nile valley. He was offered a salary of a little over £50 a year, or US$250. The money was relatively unimportant; Carter had found a niche where he could establish himself and build a reputation. Successful archaeologists, he had no doubt noticed, tended to acquire respect, honours and wealth. The idea of travelling to a hot and exotic land like Egypt must also have held attractions for a young man.

Newberry may have voiced his concern that Carter would not fit in with the public school set that dominated the British social scene in Egypt at the time, because he received a letter from Professor Griffith of Oxford University which included the following: '. . . if you come across a colourist who would like a trip to Egypt for expenses paid and nothing else . . . it matters not whether the artist is a gentleman . . .'[4] However, if Carter imagined he was leaving a society where he felt constantly inferior and 'put in his place' by people he knew were no brighter or more hard working than him in favour of somewhere more egalitararian he must have been grievously disappointed to discover that the expatriate community in Egypt was possibly even more rigidly class conscious than the British Museum had been.[5]

To begin with it was an unhappy time for Carter. Originating from the background he did, his initiation into the upper echelons of society was not an easy one. In addition, Carter could be, at times, rather rude, aggressive and extremely obstinate. Consequently, he often found himself ostracized amongst his colleagues. Even so, by late 1891 Carter was ready for his first excursion to Egypt. As the youngest among a generation of new archaeologists, and without any professional qualifications, he boarded ship for Alexandria. 'How well I remember the depressed state of mind I was in when I left Victoria Station, and the nostalgia of the young and inexperienced when I crossed the Channel and found myself alone for the first time in a foreign country, the tongue of which I had no practical knowledge.'[6]

Not comfortable and probably not capable of socializing with his colleagues and superiors, Carter went his own way in Egypt, thereby confirming the suspicions of the expatriate community that he was not, and never would be, 'one of them'. Carter instead headed for the shade of the local cafés, where he would sit for hours drinking coffee and smoking with the 'natives', as they were dismissively referred to by the Europeans. No doubt he cut a distinctive figure among the flowing robes and the headdresses of the locals, wearing the regulation three-piece suit and tie that all expatriate Englishmen sported in those days (with the exception of one or two notorious eccentrics such as Lawrence of Arabia). Carter hated the way the

British looked down on the Egyptians, lumping them together in a stereotype summarized by Professor Ayad al-Qazzaz as, 'dirty, dishonest, unscrupulous, inferior, backward, primitive, savage, sensual, over-sexed, half-naked, fatalistic, lazy, unambitious, shifty, scheming.' Having been looked down on himself, by the same people, Carter knew that such attitudes derived from ignorance and arrogance.[7]

Mixing with the despised local people was a shrewder move than Carter probably realized at first. Not only did his new friends in the cafés teach him to speak Arabic, they also taught him about the tombs and the illicit but profitable antique market which had depended on them for so many centuries. Some members of this street café society belonged to the El-Rassul family from the village of Querna next to the Valley of the Kings. They were a dynasty of tomb robbers and proud of their heritage, despite the fact that the government was keen to stop them plying their trade.

There is a story, recounted by Nicholas Reeves and Richard Wilkinson in their book, *The Complete Valley of the Kings*, that the El-Rassul family was responsible for the stunning discovery in the mid nineteenth century of a tomb containing the mummified remains and funerary equipment of fifty royal figures including Tuthmosis III, Sethos I and Ramesses II. There are a number of versions of the tale but the favourite one is that a member of the family lost a goat down a hidden tomb shaft; when he clambered down to rescue the animal he found himself in an Aladdin's cave of treasures. The family, it is said, lived happily off the proceeds of this discovery for several years until experts in the West noticed how many important papyri and artefacts were suddenly appearing on the market from an unknown source and an official investigation was launched.[8]

Accordingly, the authorities vigorously pursued the El-Rassul family both day and night. It is even said that two senior members of the family were cruelly tortured, one of whom was never seen again. Despite such blatant brutality on the part of the Egyptian government the El-Rassul held strong and refused to divulge their secret. Later, however, realizing the impossible position his people were in, the head of the family decided it was the time to 'cut their losses and claim a reward for telling the authorities where they had found the tomb, full of treasure, rather than trying to empty it further with officials dogging their every step.'[9] Subsequently, in the summer of 1881 the Egyptian Antiquities Service, led by Emile Brugsch, was taken to the hiding place and, at last, the burial place of Egypt's royal dead was finally uncovered.

The inhabitants of the Valley of the Kings claimed a heritage as old as the pharaohs themselves. Tomb robbery was in their blood and despite the fact that they had not received any formal kind of education, they knew where to find the most sought after artefact and if not, they knew where to get one made. Carter soon realized that he could exploit the situation for his own good. With his professional rivals loath to have any contact with the locals, after all there were mere 'natives', Carter positively encouraged such a relationship. As a result, it was unlikely that any deal he struck with the indigenous tomb robbers would ever be reported back to his employers. As luck would have it, the El-Rassul were to become his faithful henchmen throughout his time in Egypt, supplying him with contacts, information and a workforce he could rely on to be discreet.[10]

The driving force in Egyptian archaeology at this time was William Flinders Petrie, the first Edward's Professor of Egyptology at University College, London. At the time of his first meeting with

Carter, Petrie was preparing to dig at the city of Amarna, coincidentally the city founded by Tutankhamun's father, Akhenaten. Little
did Carter realize how intertwined in his own life these characters
from past and present would become.[11] Carter would later become
assistant to Petrie, joining him in Amarna in early in 1892. However,
his first job was in Upper Egypt, under the direction of Percy
Newberry, recording the scenes and inscriptions in the thirty-nine
rock-cut tombs of Beni Hasan. Carter was an excellent worker, who
paid meticulous attention to detail, but ironically Petrie was less
than impressed by his efforts. In his journal for the period 3–9
January 1892, Petrie records, 'Mr Carter is a good-natured lad, whose
interest is entirely in painting and natural history ... it is of no use
to me to work him up as an excavator.'[12]

This must rate as one of the great misjudgements of history, up
there with the record companies that turned down the Beatles half a
century later or Neville Chamberlain waving his piece of paper and
announcing 'peace in our time' after meeting Hitler. But, underestimated by Flinders Petrie, Carter was beginning to dream dreams
and make plans that an academic couldn't begin to comprehend.
Because of his training in art, Carter would have made an excellent
forger, capable of producing exact copies of any originals placed
before him. This skill made him useful to Petrie, and would later
stand Carter in excellent stead in his quest for fame and fortune.
Determined to succeed despite his educational and imaginative
deficiencies, Carter patiently absorbed the basics of hieroglyphics
and learned everything that the distinguished men around him
could teach him about archaeology and Egyptology, awaiting his
opportunity to move forward.

Nine years after leaving England his patience and efforts were
rewarded and he was appointed by Gaston Maspero (later Sir

Gaston) to the post of Inspector of Monuments in Upper Egypt and Nubia, based in Luxor close to the Valley of the Kings. There can be little doubt that he owed his appointment to the Swiss Egyptologist Edouard Naville, who was not only a good friend of Maspero, but had for the past six years worked with and observed Carter's activity in Thebes. Maspero, who was Director General of the Egyptian Service of Antiquities, disagreed with Flinders Petrie about Carter's talents. He was also a firm supporter of the rights of foreigners to dig in the Valley of the Kings, believing that without their money and self-discipline, the wonders of the tombs would all eventually fall prey to families like the El-Rassul.

While working as an inspector for Maspero, Carter was also employed by an American multimillionaire from Rhode Island, Theodore M. Davis. Davis had made his money in finance and law and now wanted to indulge himself in the most expensive hobby of all, treasure hunting. Like many rich men he liked wintering in the pleasant climate of Luxor, sailing up and down the Nile on his houseboat, *Bedawin*, with his companion, Mrs Emma B. Andrews, but he had found he needed a stimulating pastime to distract him from all the tranquillity in the life.[15]

'He often told me,' Carter later wrote of Davis, 'that he would like to have some active interest during his sojourns in Upper Egypt. Thus ... I put the following proposition to him. The Egyptian Government would be willing, when my duties permitted, for me to carry out researches in the Valley of the tombs of the Kings on his behalf, if he would be willing on his part to cover the costs thereof, that the Egyptian Government in return for his generosity would be pleased, whenever it was possible, to give him any duplicate antiquities resulting from these researches. At the same time, I told him of my conjecture regarding the possibility of discovering the Tomb of Tuthmosis IV . . .'[14]

In 1902 Davis was granted a concession to excavate in the Valley of the Kings 'under Government supervision', and Carter was instructed by Maspero to oversee the wealthy amateur. He found Davis to be an open-minded, yet determined, man to work with and was recorded as saying, 'There is conspicuously more to him than is found in most of the millionaire diggers'.[15] Davis was quite willing to allow Carter to nominate the sites worthy of investigation, and to supervise the digging. It almost appeared that Davis was not the least concerned about finding anything or not. It was the hunt itself which he enjoyed. To Carter's utter dismay, all standard archaeological practices were abandoned as no recording, let alone conservation, was carried out on any item that Davis uncovered. Despite such wholly unsystematic procedures, Carter needed a patron and Davis needed an expert.

Despite his haphazard methods, Davis made a number of good finds, although nothing that would add greatly to his already considerable fortune. Working with the British archaeologist Edward Ayrton, he found the tombs of Tuthmosis IV, King Siptah and Queen Hatshepsut among others, but they were bare by the time he got to them apart from the odd piece of furniture.

As well as working for Maspero and Davis, Carter must also have been developing interests of his own with the El-Rassul, which none of his colleagues knew anything about, buying and selling antiquities on their behalf and threading his way through the maze of underground chambers and corridors between tombs. Carter's official career, however, was about to end abruptly.

One evening in 1905, he received a message from his old employer

Sir William Flinders Petrie, asking for assistance. Petrie was at the time recording hieroglyphs in a tomb at Saqqara and was living, along with his wife and three young female apprentices, in a camp near the site. On 8 January a group of French tourists had arrived and, when told they needed tickets to enter the tomb, had become abusive towards the local inspectors and guards. Mostly the worse for drink, having spent the previous hour or so at the Service's Rest House, all but three of them had bought tickets. At the entrance of the monument, the accompanying inspector requested to see who had tickets and who had not. However, the party would not wait for the inspector, but rushed at the door and forced it open by breaking one of the side catches, which held the padlock. Upon finding that there were no candles with which to see anything, they rushed back out again, roughly handled the inspector and demanded their money back. One of the visitors struck a guard, which consequently led to an all-out brawl.

Upon hearing the news, Carter immediately rounded up a squad of Egyptian guards and was soon on the scene. After exchanging a few angry remarks with the French visitors he ordered the guards to protect themselves and, in the ensuing bedlam, one of the Frenchmen was knocked to the ground.

There is no doubt that Carter had dealt with the troublemakers in a less than diplomatic and polite manner and a few days later an official complaint was lodged against him with Sir Gaston Maspero. In the interests of calming troubled waters, Maspero asked Carter to make an apology so that the whole incident could be put to one side and everyone continue with their work. It was a simple if irritating request which could easily have been complied with.[16]

Carter, however, feeling that he was entirely in the right and the

Frenchmen in the wrong, stubbornly refused to cooperate, insisting that it was they not he who should apologize. But the French were officially in charge of the archaeological sites of Egypt, a hangover from the period, over a century before, when Napoleon Bonaparte had invaded the country. Although he sympathized with his employee, Maspero knew that if Carter couldn't be persuaded to compromise he would have to be sacrificed for political reasons. Maspero fully appreciated the valuable work that Carter was doing and didn't want to lose him. In fact, he told one colleague that he couldn't imagine how they would manage without Carter. He repeatedly begged him to rethink his position, and wrote to Carter's friends asking them to intercede on his behalf as well, but Carter would not budge. His colleague Newberry reported, 'Carter refused to give it [an apology], saying that he had only done his duty and, as a result of his refusal, he had to resign his post.'[17]

In the end the reluctant Maspero had no choice but to dismiss Carter from his post. It must have seemed to everyone that this was the most terrible blow for a man who already viewed himself as an outsider and whose only hope of social and financial advancement was through his work. If he had been an angry and resentful man before, this would surely have been enough to cement those resentments for ever. It is possible however that the incident was not all it seemed and that Carter refused to apologize from some ulterior motive; it seems unlikely that a man who stood to lose so much would have refused to make such a small concession to diplomacy. Perhaps Carter was, in the modern idiom, 'working to a different agenda'. Maybe he needed to be free of the Antiquities Service in order to do something bigger, something bolder, something very secret indeed; and he knew perfectly well that, because of his connections with the El-Rassul, he would be able to support himself without the meagre salary which the Antiquities Service had been paying him.

Perhaps the drunken Frenchmen inadvertently gave him an opportunity to leave his job while at the same time appearing to be a man of high principles. He may have exasperated Maspero and his other colleagues with his stubbornness, but he did not lose their respect. It could, in fact, be argued that he was acting with more integrity and dignity than they were by refusing to apologize for an offence he did not believe he had committed. If the incident had not occurred and he had merely handed in his notice, they might have asked questions about what else he might be planning. As it was, they thought they could understand his motivations, even if they didn't agree with them.

Although he faced an uncertain future, there was never the slightest danger that Carter would return to England. In fact, he moved back to Luxor where, according to Charles Breasted, he was offered hospitality by none other than the chief guard held responsible for the tomb robberies by the El-Rassul family, who had been subsequently dismissed.[18] For the next four years he did whatever he could to bring in an income. He returned to his first love, painting, and sold his wares to the rich guests staying in the Winter Palace Hotel, Luxor. He also worked as a freelance draughtsman for Theodore Davis, recording the objects uncovered in the tombs of Yuya and Tjuya. It was not a happy time for Carter.

He must also have had a great deal of time on his hands to sit around in the cafés and cultivate his friendships with the El-Rassul and other locals. It was known that about this time he started to deal in the odd antiquity and work of art, no doubt acting as a go-between for the dealers and tourists. Visitors to Egypt might well be wary of buying articles offered to them in broken English by swarthy men or smiling boys in Arab dress, but if their guide, a man dressed in a suit and tie who they knew to be an expert in such matters, told them that it was safe to buy, they would feel far more comfortable. He was, in other words 'a gentleman dealer', acting on behalf of a number of foreign buyers and taking 15 per cent for his efforts. Contacts made during his employment as an inspector proved useful.[19]

In 1900 two local men, by the names of Macarios and Andraos, approached Carter, and proposed a deal to him. They had recently discovered a tomb, number KV34, and, in return for paying the cost of clearance, they would get to keep a share of the discoveries. Having pushed through an agreement with the authorities, when Carter himself had been an inspector, that 'either half value or half antiquities shall be the finder's property', Carter had no reason to decline their offer. The man in charge of the clearance, who was later to become Carter's trusted aide, was Ahmed Girigar. This obviously opened the door to prospective skulduggery with his trusted 'natives'. Carter got in touch with dealers in Luxor, announcing every so often that he had something of interest to sell. None of his customers ever reported themselves disappointed by the items he brought them.[20]

These were Carter's wilderness years, a time when his exact movements were unclear. To all intents and purposes, by leaving his inspector's post, he had become invisible to the world and could, as a result, do more or less as he pleased. The perceived wisdom until now has been that these were difficult times for Carter but they were perhaps also very exciting. Having discovered more about his later life, we might conclude that he concentrated harder on cultivating his local contacts and building up the trading side of his activities in this period than has previously been thought. So many plans must have been fermenting in his mind, as he awaited an opportunity to put them into action.

Although it is likely Carter was making more money during this period than has been generally supposed, he was not yet building the sort of fortune needed to finance the work he really wanted to do. For that he still needed a major sponsor, someone as rich or richer than Theodore Davis, but someone who was of a like mind to him, someone who would be on his wavelength.

Despite his undoubted annoyance with Carter for his stubbornness, Maspero must have had considerable admiration for the principled stand the young man had taken and maybe even some affection for someone who he could see was an outsider and a less than contented soul. When the opportunity arose to introduce Carter to someone who might be able to help him restart his career, Maspero jumped at it. He introduced Carter to the Earl of Carnarvon, via Lord Cromer. This was the answer to all Carter's secret dreams. It was a fortuitous meeting for both of them.

4

The Earl of Carnarvon – 'Lordy' of all he Surveys

*Carnarvon ... was of medium height and slight in build, with
nondescript features and sparse hair. The shape of his head was
abnormal, flattened on top, sloping abruptly downward, and widened,
which gave a curious effect on a slender neck ... The unhealthy colour
of his complexion was made more conspicuous by the fact that his
face was pitted from smallpox. But when he discussed Egyptology,
his pale, lustreless eyes lit up with enthusiasm ...*[1]

Joseph Lindon Smith

The Fifth Earl of Carnarvon was born on 26 June 1866 in Hampshire.
The only son of the reigning Earl, he suceeded to the title in 1890.
Blessed with every possible opportunity in a golden age of aristoc-
racy, he had never managed to find any useful way to utilize his
considerable charm, intelligence and good looks to do anything
other than lead an amusing life. He was described by one writer of
the time as 'a cross between Max Beerbohm's Duke of Dorset and P.
G. Wodehouse's Bertie Wooster'.[2]

His father, the fourth earl, had been a more formidable achiever;
a member of Disraeli's cabinet and highly respected by all who
came into contact with him. The family owned a stately home in
England called Highclere Castle which was considered one of the

finest in the land with rolling lawns, cedar trees and lakes outside the windows, a great library and walls covered with old masters inside. As well as priceless collections of books and pictures there was also the furniture, including Napoleon's desk and chair, which added to the family fortune. With 36,000 acres of countryside, containing stud farms and pastures, it was an enormous estate by anyone's standards.[3]

Little of his father's seriousness and scholarly approach to life rubbed off on the son. Known as 'Porchy' to his friends, he attended Eton as a young boy and achieved nothing. He then attended Cambridge University but was more often at the races than at lectures. Consequently, there is no record of his graduation. However, he was extremely wealthy and powerful in the way that English lords of that period could be. His generosity to friends, relatives and servants was legendary. He was handsome and amusing and could think of nothing he wanted to do more with his life beyond travelling the world and playing sport. At the age of twenty-one he sailed round the world and led the life of an aristocratic playboy. As such, he became an occasional companion to Queen Victoria's eldest son, the fast-living Prince of Wales. A report in *Autocar* magazine described him 'like a flash, whizzing past pedestrians and cyclists at a terrifying speed of up to twenty miles an hour.'[4]

Porchy inherited the Earldom in 1889 at the age of twenty-three. But with so much of his wealth tied up in land, and with a great house to maintain, Carnarvon desperately needed a cash boost to support his chosen lifestyle. As a result, on his twenty-ninth birthday he married Almina Victoria Maris Wombell. She appears to have been a beautiful and intelligent young girl who had the added advantage of being the natural child of Baron Rothschild, one of the richest men in the world. It is said that on their wedding day he presented the happy couple with a cheque for £250,000 as a gift.

At that time the Rothschild dynasty was by far the richest and most powerful family in the world. Of German Jewish origin, they had propped up any number of governments with loans far in excess of anything any other private fortune could manage. They were at the very centre of world power and Carnarvon's connection to them would have increased his influence a thousandfold. He and Almina had two children: Henry, Viscount Porchester and Lady Evelyn Herbert who later became her father's closest friend and travelling companion.[5]

The relationship between Carnarvon's family and the Rothschilds went back to 1847 when Baron Rothschild became the first Jew elected to the British parliament. Because he wouldn't repeat the words in the parliamentary oath, 'the one true faith of a Christian', Rothschild was barred from taking his seat. There was a furious reaction, which the then Lord Carnarvon defused by suggesting that the Commons simply abolish by resolution any disqualification against an individual elected to parliament. It worked and the two men became close friends, culminating in an alliance of the families with the marriage of the fifth earl and Almina.[6]

While in his thirties, Carnarvon was involved in a motoring accident in Germany, resulting in his chest being crushed, his jaw broken and his limbs badly burned. His heart had actually stopped beating but his chauffeur dragged him from the wreckage, had the initiative to throw cold water over him and the shock revived him. Carnarvon's health never fully recovered from the experience and he was almost constantly in pain from then on. His weight dropped below nine stone and refused to go up however hard Carnarvon worked at it. His doctor advised him to travel abroad for the winters in order to avoid the cold and damp of the English climate. An inveterate traveller, Carnarvon was no doubt happy to comply. In 1903 he visited Egypt for the first time. The climate was perfect for him, but, like Theodore Davis, he found Cairo rather dull after the cities of Europe and America. He looked around for distractions and, as many other intelligent gentlemen of leisure had done before him, became interested in the idea of digging for treasure. He moved himself to the Winter Palace Hotel in Luxor which would become a home from home in the coming years and enquired about the possibilities of being granted a concession to dig.[7]

With an immense fortune at his fingertips, Carnarvon was in a position to do more or less as he pleased. According to his own testimony, in an uncompleted article written just before his death, he was instantly fascinated by digging. 'It had always been my wish and intention as far back as 1889 to start excavating, but for one reason or another I had never been able to begin.'[8] Carnarvon contacted the British Consul-General in Egypt, through his friend Lord Cromer, and was granted a licence to dig in an area of Sheikh Abd el-Qurna. Ironically, this particular site lay upon a plateau above the valley where Carter had lived while working for Edouard Naville. His team of diggers had scarcely been operating for twenty-four hours when they struck what appeared to be an untouched burial pit. 'This gave rise to much excitement in the Antiquities Department, which soon simmered down when the pit was found to be unfinished,' Carnarvon reported. 'There, for six weeks, enveloped in a cloud of dust, I stuck to it day in and day out. Beyond finding a large mummified cat in its case, which now graces the Cairo Museum, nothing whatsoever rewarded my strenuous and very dusty endeavour. This utter failure, however, instead of disheartening me had the effect of making me keener than ever.'[9]

Despite such failure Carnarvon decided he needed to convince the authorities to give him another chance. Once more he contacted his friend Lord Cromer asking for advice on obtaining a more rewarding concession. Cromer went back to Maspero, who, after thoughtful consideration, decided it would be prudent to seek the services of an expert excavator. The man he suggested was none other than the highly respected Howard Carter. After years in the wilderness, there could have been no better outcome for the ambitious archaeologist. He had found the patron, and the friend, he so patently needed. In addition, Carnarvon was as delighted by the introduction as Carter was. Now, at last, he had found the man who would put the stamp of academic respectability on his lordship's amateur endeavours.[10]

While he was undoubtedly at the apex of the social pyramid of the time, no one could ever accuse Carnarvon of being snobbish in his choice of friends. In fact, he had something of a reputation for recruiting 'quaint' people from all walks of life into his circle. The fact that Carter was 'not a gentleman' would not have worried him in the least; Carnarvon was above such petty considerations. In fact, he might even have liked Carter the more for his lack of social graces. He could see that Carter had the knowledge that he needed, was hungry for success and willing to work incredibly hard. The two men fired one another's imaginations and began to dream big dreams.

While Carnarvon's health improved a little, he never regained the robustness he had enjoyed before his accident. He frequently had to retire to his bed to rest and Carter described him as looking 'ten years older than he was'. His marriage to Almina also became strained; perhaps she felt replaced in his affections by the seductive tombs of the ancient pharaohs.

Carter by now knew exactly what he wanted to do in the Valley of the Kings while Carnarvon had the influence to make things happen and the resources to pay for as many men as Carter needed, which would at times be many hundreds. Carnarvon also had the connections to smooth the path of whatever venture they might decide to embark on together. If Carter had the local contacts and knew how to get hold of great antiquities, Carnarvon certainly knew what to do with them. If he didn't add them to his own fast-growing collection, he knew exactly who to sell them to, whether it was museum curators with apparently bottomless acquisition budgets, or private collectors like the famous Middle East oil broker, 'Mr Five Percent', Calouste Gulbenkian. Carter was dazzled by a man who was so effortlessly everything that he was not and yet who was happy to treat him as an equal. Carnarvon must have exercised all his considerable charm and Carter was duly captivated. They became partners and over the coming years Carter started to ape his friend and mentor, wearing the same sort of heavy tweed clothes no matter how great the heat, and sporting a homburg hat and a cigarette holder.

The two of them would ideally have liked to start work in the Valley of the Kings, but Theodore Davis, Carter's erstwhile employer, still held the concession there. Carter and Carnarvon had to look elsewhere, and at the same time busied themselves building Carnarvon's already impressive collection of Egyptian artefacts with the help of the El-Rassul. Not only could Carter get hold of the best pieces, he had also developed excellent judgement on what was good and beautiful and what was worthless. However, Davis remained a huge problem: he was digging where they wanted to be and was in grave danger of finding the treasure which Carter was certain still lay there waiting to be found. In 1906 Davis had discovered under a rock a small cup which carried the throne name of Tutankhamun. With the help of his English archaeologist, Edward Ayrton, he then discovered something the following year which he was sure was a tomb.

'At the depth of twenty-five feet,' Davis wrote, 'we found a room filled almost to the top with dried mud, showing that water had entered it.' Further investigations revealed 'a broken box containing several pieces of gold leaf stamped with the names of Tutankhamun and his wife.'[11]

Over the following days more finds surfaced. None were spectacular and none indicated that the tomb of Tutankhamun might be nearby. What had been unearthed, however, were embalming jars, most probably those that had been used in the embalming of the young king. After much discussion, the assembly of sizeable jars was taken carefully to Davis's house in the valley and, with much pomp and ceremony, they were officially opened to the excited congregation. One by one the contents were carefully removed, to reveal a number of clay seal impressions, with the name of Tutankhamun inscribed upon them, a collection of linen fragments, together with an assortment of broken crockery and bones. With his usual disregard for proper archaeological modus operandi, Davis proceeded to demonstrate to his guests just how strong ancient linen was by ripping the papyrus covers to shreds! Carter and Carnarvon could only sit by helplessly and witness these deplorable antics. Nonetheless, they would eventually have the last laugh at Davis's expense. His find was subsequently revealed to have originated in the entrance corridor to Tutankhamun's tomb.

In 1912, Davis claimed that the pit he had found was the actual tomb of the young king and declared that the Valley of the Kings was now exhausted. But Carter was sure he was wrong. How could such a modest tomb be the resting place of any pharaoh? Even one as apparently insignificant as Tutankhamun. So, while watching the American's every move in the valley, Carter and Carnarvon grudgingly worked on in other places, no doubt living in fear that each day they would hear that Theodore Davis, a man they considered a vulgar interloper, had unearthed the last great find of the valley.

Their own efforts produced mixed results. Their first season together, Carnarvon extended his Theban concession and applied for another at Aswan. 'I thought I would have two strings,' he was reported as saying, 'as I am not sure I will get my wife to stay another whole two months at Luxor.' On an earlier occasion he wrote, 'If I get what I want I shall bring out a learned man as I have no time to learn all the requisite data.' This 'learned man' was Howard Carter.[12]

In 1907 Carnarvon obtained his concession to excavate in a more promising area at the northern end of the Theban necropolis. Under the supervision of Carter, he didn't have to wait long for a successful outcome. After only two weeks of digging the excavation team uncovered the decorated tomb of Tetiky, a mayor of Thebes during the early part of the Eighteenth Dynasty. This was soon followed by another tomb containing two wooden tablets inscribed with writings of Ptahotep. One of the most important historical texts to be unearthed in Egypt, it describes the defeat of the Asiatic Hyksos, who invaded Egypt during the Seventeenth Dynasty, by King Kamose. More important discoveries ensued, including the two lost temples of Queen Hatshepsut and Ramesses IV. With contributions from Carter, Carnarvon published, in 1912, a massive report of their findings entitled *Five Years Exploration at Thebes, a Record of Work Done 1907–1911*. Receiving the critical acclaim it so rightly deserved, Carnarvon could now add to this the commendation of his Egyptological colleagues.

Despite their successes both Carnarvon and Carter wanted to broaden their outlook beyond the boundaries of the Theban necropolis. They decided to extend their activities to Sakha, ancient Xois, in the Delta. Whether any finds were uncovered or not is difficult to ascertain as reports of the excavations were never published. In addition, after only two weeks work the site was rapidly abandoned 'on account of the number of cobras and cerastes [horned vipers] that infested the whole area'.[13] The following season they transferred their operation to the site of Tell el-Balamun, an ancient settlement located some nineteen kilometres from the Mediterranean coast. The finds were meagre, just a few small inscribed bracelets dating from the Graeco-Roman period.

Their frustrating efforts during that year were described by Carnarvon in a publication in 1912. 'Open and half-filled mummy pits, heaps of rubbish, great mounds of rock debris with, here and there, fragments of coffins and shreds of mummy wrappings protruding from the sand ... Evidence of the explorers and robbers present themselves at every turn.'[14]

While they must have been holding their breath for fear that Davis might find the tomb of Tutankhamun before they had a chance to return to the valley, Carter and Carnarvon often used to joke to people in England about how they were duping the rich American, whom Carnarvon actively disliked, by sending him on any number of wild goose chases. They also frequently spoke of how they had managed to make money at Davis's expense.

During those early years in their relationship, while they were apparently engaged in scholarly and unprofitable excavations, Carter and Carnarvon were, in fact, making a great deal of money out of their activities in Egypt. It was Carter's idea that they should buy antiquities and sell them at a profit. They knew the British Museum and the Metropolitan Museum of Art in New York were always on the lookout for Egyptian artefacts, as were many other museums and private collectors, and they were in a prime position to supply them. The profits they made could go towards subsidizing further excavations.[15]

Carnarvon and Carter worked as a team; under Carter's guidance Carnarvon began to assemble his great Egyptian collection. He said, 'my chief aim was then, and is now, not merely to buy something because it is rare, but rather to consider the beauty of an object than its pure historic value'.[16] Many of these so-called 'beautiful objects' would also find their way into other major museum collections, with Carter often taking a profit as the vendor as well as an agent's commission on the sale.[17] On top of his salary of £200 a month from Carnarvon, Carter must have made a tidy sum, although what is not known is where Carter had obtained the artefacts in the first instance. Suspicion would lie, once more, at the door of the El-Rassul family.

Experts have estimated that on one deal alone Carter earned enough money to live in comfort for the next ten years. That particular sale involved the Treasure of the Three Princesses, a huge collection of jewellery dating from the Eighteenth Dynasty. Following the contents of Tutankhamun's tomb, it is considered by many Egyptologists to be the finest discovery to come out of the Theban necropolis. It first came to light in 1914 after a huge rainstorm had battered the ancient burial ground known as the Cemetery of the Apes. Contrary to popular opinion, flash floods are common in Egypt and were greeted with much enthusiasm by the local tomb raiders. Violent surges of water would regularly flush hidden treasures out of the rocks or loosen the sands to reveal new clues about concealed hoards. In his book entitled *Tutankhamun: The Untold Story*, Thomas Hoving states that, 'when this particular storm commenced the El-Rassul set out from their home in Qurna to search in the crevices of the mountains. They struck it rich as a fabulous cache of jewels were flushed out of their hiding place by the waters, almost literally falling into their hands.'[18] Rumours of the find spread quickly to the ears of a well-known local dealer, Muhammed Mohassib, who offered the El-Rassul a generous fee for their plunder. For safekeeping, the treasure was then divided among his family members, Mohassib knowing that it would not be long before the world's collectors came knocking at his door.

In the West the desire for Egyptian artefacts was intensifying together with an increase in prices. In 1912 Carnarvon wrote to Wallis Budge at the British Museum: 'You have heard, of course, that Morgan had bought the Coptic MSS you refused for £80,000.'[19] This was an astounding sum of money yet even small pieces were now changing hands for thousands of pounds. Although Budge was an assistant keeper at the British Museum, he was also an avid private collector and would regularly visit Egypt on buying trips. It could be argued that he used his position at the British Museum for his own personal gain. Consequently, his methods were often described as shameful and offensive by the British and French officials.

Carter was now perfectly set up to act as middle man between the local dealers and the great museums and collectors who were in contact with Carnarvon. In 1917 he started buying the Three Princesses' jewels from Mohassib. The deals went on for the next five

years as he bought up one batch after another of the cunningly
rationed treasures with Carnarvon's money. Carter then went to the
Metropolitan Museum and told them that Carnarvon was willing to
sell most of the collection on to them, using Carter as the agent. The
museum was delighted and happy to buy through Carter, who then
became as adept as any Egyptian dealer at playing the museums
and collectors off against one another, with the Metropolitan always
coming out the winner. He offered them the hoard in small tempting
lots, as and when he was able to get them from Mohassib, to ensure
the highest possible price. By 1922 the Metropolitan Museum had
paid £53,397 – several million pounds by today's prices – and owned
a total of 225 pieces of jewellery from the Three Princesses find.
Everyone was more than happy with the results of the long years of
deals, particularly Carter, who no longer had to give a second
thought to his financial future.[20]

The machinations of Carter and Carnarvon over the sale of the
jewellery are well documented, but there must have been many
other smaller deals taking place through which Carnarvon was able
to increase his collection, which was growing all the time. But the
money they were making from the treasure of the Three Princesses
and other small deals on the side during those years was nothing
compared to what they were already stealing from somewhere else
and starting to introduce, very subtly, into the marketplace.[21]

Carnarvon's holding of Egyptian art from private purchases and
excavations was steadily becoming one of the finest private collections in the world. Some referred to it as his 'pocket collection',
implying that his lordship was merely filling his pockets with the
treasures as he found them, taking advantage of his diplomatic
immunity to help himself to anything that took his fancy. In fact, he
did not behave any differently to the great museums. Plunder was

the name of the game and grave robbing the norm. If you had money and influence you bribed corrupt officials and steamrollered the objections of those who tried in vain to stop the vandalism. The only defence that the museums could put forward was that if they didn't do it, other less reputable people would. If museums didn't grab as many of the artefacts as possible, they would disappear from sight into the vaults of private collectors and dealers, never to be enjoyed by the public. It was far better that the priceless treasures be properly cleaned, listed and displayed for all to admire than fall into the hands of a few wealthy individuals, to be seen by only an elite few and peddled to the highest bidder. There was clearly some validity to this argument but it was nevertheless the wholesale plundering of one nation's heritage by powerful foreign interests.[22]

It has been suggested that Howard Carter had been knowingly profiteering from tomb robbery even before he met Lord Carnarvon. As early as 1900, when he was Inspector General of Antiquities in Upper Egypt, he unearthed a tomb containing a relief sculpture of Queen Tiye. According to Carter he simply photographed the piece and the tomb was then closed. But this was not the end of the matter. In 1908, the new Inspector, Arthur Weigall, decided to reopen the tomb. To his amazement, he discovered that the relief had vanished and in its place was a huge gaping hole in the wall. Not wanting to point the finger of blame at Carter, he concluded that in the interim period robbers had entered the tomb and removed the beautiful carving. However, the relief subsequently turned up at the Royal Museum in Brussels, with its original hieroglyphic inscription crudely obscured by Greek characters to disguise its true nature. Even though there was no evidence that Carter was directly involved, the coincidences are significant.

Although Carnarvon was generally a popular figure, there were

always those who were voicing their doubts about his suitability
as an excavator. Weigall described the earl as an odd mixture of
Bohemian and plutocrat.

> A man who has seen a great deal of the underworld and is
> reputed to have pitted his brains against and outwitted the
> toughest bookies and "crooks" on the turf. He is an adventurous
> soul who goes his own way and seems to care not a jot for
> public opinion. His manners are notoriously bad: he is often
> thought to be insolent; and yet, in spite of many disadvantages
> he manages generally to attain his objects, and is regarded
> with affection by his friends. I do not know whether he is
> consistently cunning, or often ingenuous.[23]

Weigall considered neither Carnarvon nor Carter to be scholars, but
conceded that Carter was an expert fieldworker who knew as much
as any man about the handling of antiquities. He believed that both
men were extremely casual and tactless and had already aroused
much 'native hostility'.[24] Whatever hostility they might have stirred
up at that stage was nothing compared to the whirlwind which was
to come.

5

THE OFFICIAL STORY
OF THE DISCOVERY

'Can you see anything?' Carnarvon
'Yes, wonderful things.' Carter [1]

In 1914 Davis finally gave up his hunt for Tutankhamun in the Valley
of the Kings. When he stopped digging he was just a few feet away
from the tomb, but the dig had reached the edge of a roadway and
Carter persuaded Davis that if he went any further there was a serious
danger he would undermine the road. Davis, perhaps finally tiring of
the chase, agreed and called a halt to the proceedings. He died the
following year; perhaps his declining health had also helped Carter
persuade him that it was time to give up the expensive search in an
area which Davis himself had already said he thought exhausted.

War was breaking out in Europe and the pursuit of relics in Egypt
seemed of less relevance to the general public than ever before. The
attention of the authorities and the media was directed towards
matters of defence and survival. Although in some ways this was
restricting, it also enabled Carter and Carnarvon to operate with
greater freedom and without attracting undue attention. They took
up the concession as soon as Davis gave it up and Carter began to
work systematically across the area, certain that there was still at
least one great tomb to be uncovered – that of Tutankhamun.

When Turkey declared war on the Allies in the same year, Britain announced that Egypt – nominally still part of the Turkish empire – would be placed under the protection of His Majesty and would henceforth constitute a British protectorate. Realizing that the British were fully stretched fighting on the Western Front and in various other theatres throughout the world, the Turks attempted the following year to reassert their authority over Egypt and the Nile. The British turned them back but, when the Ottoman army in turn defeated the Allies at Gallipoli, the Turks followed up their victory with a second invasion of Egypt in 1916. Once again the British rebuffed them and then overran the Sinai Peninsula, attacked Palestine and permanently removed the Turkish threat to Egypt.

During the war, Carnarvon was stranded for much of the time in England. But Carter, when asked about the conflict, always replied that he had served as a King's Messenger. In a sense that was true. In 1915, with his ability to speak Arabic, Carter carried secret dispatches for Sir Henry McMahon under the protection of the Foreign Office. He also carried verbal messages and acted as a translator in the course of clandestine exchanges between British and French officials and their Arab contacts.[2]

He was shocked by the cavalier way in which he saw the British treating the local workforce. Like many others who were in touch with popular local feeling, he sensed that once the war was over it would only be a matter of time before the Nationalists started to cash in on the hatred which the average Egyptian worker felt for his 'protectors'.

Carter was also dispatched to Upper Egypt to assist unofficially in policing the valley. In the confusion of war, his whereabouts during these years were shrouded in mystery and his excavations in the valley came to a virtual standstill. There is one report that some trouble, similar to the problem with the French drunks in 1903, took place leading to a dispute over army regulations. Apparently Carter stood firm in his usual self-assertive way and was dismissed from the army as a result.

In September 1917, Carter was informed that he could take indefinite leave from the army and return to digging. 'Our real campaign in the valley now opened,' he wrote. He added: 'The difficulty was to know where to begin.'[3] With a workforce of local boys and men at his disposal he began the seemingly endless task of shifting thousands of tons of rubble and sand to clear the ground down to its bedrock. There was no secret about his plan. In fact Carter was blatantly open about his activities. His belief was that he was digging in the precise area 'in which we hoped the tomb of Tutankhamun might be found.'[4] As Nicholas Reeves states in *The Complete Tutankhamun*, '. . . it was, according to all the official versions of the story, a mammoth effort of love and determination: Carnarvon continued to provide the money and Carter furnished the manpower and the management.'[5]

In the spring of 1922 Carnarvon finally tired of pouring money into Egypt. The declaration by all other Egyptologists, including the late Maspero, that the valley was truly exhausted, now also began to ring true to Carnarvon. He had made up his mind to finish with Egypt. Carter was subsequently summoned to Highclere Castle and told the digging must cease. According to Nicholas Reeves we are told that Carter was 'horrified'.[6] In a last ditch effort to convince his patron, Carter announced that, if necessary, he would finance the search himself. Although Carnarvon knew that Carter had made money as a dealer, he also knew that to hire so many workers would cost a small fortune. In addition, both parties were aware that the recently appointed Director General, Lacau, proposed to change the rules relating to compensation for 'foreign excavators'. If ever there was a time to search for the tomb of Tutankhamun it was now. Impressed with his friend's determination, Carter won a temporary reprieve – Carnarvon agreed to fund just one more season.

By the beginning of November Carter was back at work in the valley for what they both believed would be their final try. He had come across the foundations of some ancient workmen's huts which he was in the process of clearing. Spirits were low, we are told, and even Carter's optimism was apparently starting to wane. A feeling of gloom had settled over everyone; they had begun to wonder, not for the first time, if they were in fact ever going to succeed in their task.

A small water boy, however, so enthused by the idea of searching for treasure that he couldn't bring himself to shelter from the midday sun like all the others, continued to scratch in the sand with a stick, emulating the work which he no doubt had been watching his elders do. No one took any notice of him as they rested in the shade. According to Carter's account of that day in a later book, the stick jarred against something hard beneath the surface and the little boy began to dig seriously with his hands until, a few moments later, he had unearthed a stone step. Believing that he had found what everyone was looking for, his heart thumping in his chest for fear that someone else would see what he was doing and steal the glory of the find, he quickly covered it up with sand once more 'so that no rival archaeologists would see it', and ran to find Carter.[7]

Carter immediately realized that the boy had stumbled upon something important and ordered that the steps be excavated immediately. As the workers cleared the sand and rubble, a staircase was revealed, set into the hillside. By the following afternoon twelve steps had been excavated and they had uncovered the top of a blocked doorway. The blocking was stamped with oval seals which Carter could not decipher. He later confessed that at that moment he still felt doubts, thinking the door which he was uncovering was too small to be the entrance to a king's tomb. It might just be another cache of objects, like the one found by Davis. He was certain, however, that he had found something important. There was a lintel across the top of the door under which he made a small hole and peered through with a torch. Inside was stacked with rubble, as if it had been filled in to stop anyone entering.

Although he must have been severely tempted to keep digging, he knew that he should contact Carnarvon in England first; his friend and sponsor deserved to be there for the opening of the blocking. Ordering his men to refill the steps and to guard the site in shifts until he was ready to open it, Carter returned to his house on a donkey and, the following day, sent a telegram to Highclere. 'At last have made wonderful discovery in Valley, a magnificent tomb with seals intact; re-covered same for your arrival; congratulations.'

A second cable was sent to a British archaeologist, A. R. 'Pecky' Callender, who was working on another site, inviting him to join them. Carter had worked with Pecky before and they got on well. Pecky was easy-going, practical and willing to turn his hand to anything Carter asked of him. Herbert Winlock, a later director of the Metropolitan Museum, wrote that Pecky was 'one of the few colleagues who could actually be with Carter for any length of time without going out to clear his head.'[8]

It took Carnarvon and his daughter, the beautiful twenty-year-old Lady Evelyn Herbert, two and a half weeks to get to Luxor before Carter could restart the work. Under the guidance of Pecky Callender, the workers were already clearing the stairwell once more in readiness for their arrival. Carnarvon and his daughter were taken straight from Luxor train station to the site by Carter, on the backs of donkeys. Carnarvon, not a well man, must have been exhausted after their long journey, but still he wanted to see what had been discovered. Probably Lady Evelyn was anxious about her father's health and so it was decided that they would go back to the Winter Palace in Luxor to sleep and the final few steps would be cleared the following morning.[9]

The next day the last of the clearance work revealed the whole of the blocked doorway. Now Carter could see that the seals bore the name he had been hoping to find, Tutankhamun. Excitement was rising but was somewhat dampened by the realization that there were signs that a part of the blocking had at some stage been re-closed. Had tomb robbers already been there? Would they be opening the blocking only to find another empty chamber or a scattering of worthless leftovers, the riches long since removed?

Bit by bit they removed the blocking, revealing the outline of a descending corridor which had been packed to the ceiling with limestone chips. Working like ants in the midday sun, the army of workers with their baskets had the corridor cleared by four in the afternoon. The corridor was about twelve metres long and another blocked doorway was revealed at the bottom. This too was covered with seals and had signs of reclosure. They still had no way of knowing what they were going to find behind it. Would there be another staircase? Another corridor? An empty storage room or the greatest collection of forgotten royal wealth in Egypt?

Eventually, when the corridor was completely empty and the workers had returned to the surface, four people remained: Carter, Carnarvon, Lady Evelyn and Pecky Callender. They waited in tense silence as Carter made a small hole in the second blocking. When the hole was large enough he held up a candle to check there were no foul gases. Carter later wrote:

> I inserted the candle and peered in, Lord Carnarvon, Lady Evelyn and Callender standing anxiously beside me to hear the verdict. At first I could see nothing, the hot air escaping from the chamber causing the candle flame to flicker, but presently, as my eyes grew accustomed to the light, details of the room within emerged slowly from the mist, strange animals, statues and gold – everywhere the glint of gold. For the moment – an eternity it must have been to the others standing by – I was struck dumb with amazement, and when Lord Carnarvon, unable to stand the suspense any longer, inquired anxiously, 'Can you see anything?' it was all I could do to get out the words, 'Yes, wonderful things.' Then, widening the hole a little further so that both could see, we inserted an electric torch.[10]

The sight which met Carter's eyes that evening has been described a hundred times in a hundred books and publications. It is a scene which people seem never to grow tired of reading about. It is, after all, the sort of scene that all of us at one time or another have dreamed of seeing for ourselves. It was like the perfect ending to a fairy story.

For fourteen years they had dreamed of this, and for the best part of ten years these two men had laboured in the heat, Carter doing most of the labouring, Carnarvon providing an almost bottomless pit of money. They had gambled a huge part of their lives, as well as Carnarvon's fortune, on finding something which had eluded others for centuries. Now, as in all the best stories, they were receiving their reward for all those years of frustration and disappointment, for their patience and their courage in continuing where other men had given up. And their reward was a treasure trove that not only meant wealth beyond anyone's dreams, but also that they would be vindicated in the eyes of their peers. They had been proved right, the valley most certainly was not 'exhausted'.

Once the others had peered through at the wonders stacked inside, Carter set about enlarging the hole, making it big enough for all of them to see in with the help of an electric torch, flashing the beam from one amazing sight to the next.

> First, right opposite us ... were three great gilt couches, their
> sides carved in the form of monstrous animals curiously attenu-
> ated in body, as they had to be to serve their purpose, but
> heads of startling realism. Uncanny beasts enough to look upon
> at any time: seen as we saw them, their brilliant gilded surfaces
> picked out of the darkness by our electric torch, as though by
> limelight, their heads throwing grotesque distorted shadows on
> the wall behind them, they were almost terrifying.[11]

Most exciting of all, they reported when they came out, was the outline of another sealed door at the north end of the chamber, guarded on either side by two sentinels in the shape of life-sized statues of the king, dressed in gold kilts and gold sandals, armed with mace and staff, the protective sacred cobra upon their foreheads.[12] According to Christopher Frayling in *The Face of Tutankhamun*, Carter then reported:

> Presently it dawned upon our bewildered brains that in all this
> medley of objects before us there was no coffin or trace of a

mummy, and the much debated question of tomb or cache began to intrigue us afresh. With this question in view we re-examined the scene before us, and noticed for the first time that between the two black sentinel statues on the right there was a sealed doorway. The explanation gradually dawned upon us. We were but on the threshold of our discovery. What we saw was merely an antechamber. Behind the guarded door there were to be other chambers, possibly a succession of them, and in one of them beyond any shadow of doubt, in all his magnificent panoply of death, we should find the pharaoh lying.[13]

The next day Carnarvon sent a note to the Egyptologist, Alan Gardiner: 'There is enough stuff to fill the whole upstairs Egyptian section of the British Museum. I imagine it is the greatest find ever made.'[14]

That was as far as they were officially allowed to go. Before they could enter the tomb they had to have a government inspector with them. So, according to Carter, they decided to go no further that day and re-closed the hole.

'This was the day of days,' Carter wrote, 'the most wonderful that I have ever lived through, and certainly one whose like I can never hope to see again.'[15]

Later, as they talked it over, they speculated about what they might find on the other side of this third door. Would it lead them into a labyrinth of connected chambers, each one more spectacular than the last? Or might this be the only one with anything left in it, the rest stripped by robbers entering from another direction?

According to Carter, by first light they were back in the valley, working to make a hole large enough to pass through. They entered without an inspector. Once they were inside the room, which they came to call the Antechamber, and Pecky had managed to rig up electric lights, they were even more dazzled by what they saw. They wandered among the piles of artefacts, exclaiming anew at the wonders of each one and calling one another over to see what new treasures they had found.[16]

'The near-embarrassment at being intruders themselves haunted the party,' Thomas Hoving wrote in *Tutankhamun – the Untold Story*.

> An eon had passed since another human being had stood where they were standing. Yet it seemed but yesterday. Everything seemed so incredibly fresh – a bowl of mortar used in the plaster for the door, a lamp seemingly just extinguished, a fingerprint still visible on the painted surface, a remarkably well-preserved bunch of flowers left at the threshold. The intimacy of it all, the penetrating sense of life still clinging to the ancient room, made them feel like trespassers.[17]

Again, it is a picture we can all identify with. Wouldn't all of us behave in just the same way if we were ever fortunate enough to find ourselves in such a position?

Carefully examining the plasterwork between the two sentinels they concluded that the blocking must have been resealed at some time. Had ancient tomb robbers already passed this way? If so, did the Egyptian priests hastily rebuild the blocking after the thieves had gone? Although it proved that the tomb had been raided sometime during antiquity, they concluded that it probably had not been entered for the last three thousand years and certainly not through this hole. It was possible, however, that the thieves had found another entrance into whatever lay beyond.

They decided to break through this blocking and see what was on the other side. Chipping his way through the resealed section, Carter made a small hole and managed to squeeze through first, followed by Carnarvon and his daughter. Callender was a little too corpulent to get through and waited in the Antechamber for them to report back their findings.[18]

Once they were inside they knew that all their dreams had indeed come true. Before them stood an immense golden shrine and to their right an open doorway showed that there was yet another chamber filled with more glittering prizes, guarded by a reclining Anubis dog just beyond the threshold. Now Carter was confident he had found Tutankhamun and his mummy was almost certainly intact, lying deep within the shrine where he had been put to rest three thousand years before. They knew, from drawings they had seen on papyri from other tombs, that the actual body was probably encased in as many as five shrines, one within another. Inside the shrines would almost certainly be a sarcophagus containing the final gold coffins and the mummy itself.[19]

In the opinion of Thomas Hoving in *Tutankhamun: The Untold Story*, Carter and Carnarvon then decided to go back through to the Antechamber and reseal the wall where they had made the hole. That way, when they opened the tomb the following day to the outside world, everyone would have the same excitement of not knowing what might lie behind the third door. They would claim, they decided, that they had not been inside but were sure that the body of Tutankhamun lay behind the wall. Both men were supreme showmen and they wanted to make this find as dramatic and exciting as possible for the watching world. So, once they had refilled the hole, they covered up their hasty repair work with a basket and some reeds which were lying nearby.[20]

The Antechamber would be the first room they would show to the public. So, on the morning of the twenty-seventh the blocking from the entrance to the tomb was removed and Carter, for the first time, 'officially' at least, stepped into the chamber with his colleagues. Well, that's what was recorded in the official account. Four meters wide and nearly nine metres long, to the wonderment of the gathered spectators there were literally hundreds of objects piled up on top of each other. There was gold everywhere, intricate alabaster vases, ivory, semi-precious stones and six chariots stacked against a wall. Carter noticed that the chariots had their axles sawn in half so they could, no doubt, be fitted through the door at the time of burial. Everything looked exactly as it had done when the tomb had been sealed for eternity nearly three thousand years ago.

In the south-west corner of the room, where they had spotted another blocked doorway, there was a small hole in the blocking. Peering through, they could see yet another room crammed with treasures, which they would be able to access through this fourth blocked door. They called this room the Annexe. The room off the Burial Chamber they called The Treasury.

After spending most of the night moving among their various finds, they sealed up the holes and made their way home on the backs of their donkeys, no doubt all of them lost in thought.

The early entry into the Burial Chamber would probably never have been exposed until an unpublished draft of an article, written by Carnarvon, came to light. Discovered many years after the event, it not only recounted their enlargement of the hole in the second door but, in addition, it described the priceless artefacts they had seen that lay beyond. Although their midnight foray into the tomb was known to no more than the intimate circle of excavators, the world was shocked. In 1945 Alan Gardiner wrote to Percy Newberry on matters concerning the Carter material about to be presented to the Griffith Institute in Oxford, and in a postscript added: 'By the bye, did you see Lucas's article in Ann.Ser where he – to use a bit of slang – 'spilt the beans'? I am quite glad it has been done, though I couldn't have done it myself!'[21]

A month after the first entry, Alfred Lucas, the director of the Chemical Department of the Egyptian government, joined the team. Twenty five years later he wrote in an official journal, 'Les Annales du Service des Antiquités de L'Égypte': 'a considerable amount of mystery was made about the robbers' hole (the one going through to the Burial Chamber). When I first saw the tomb about December 20th, the hole was hidden by the basket work tray, or lid, and some rushes taken from the floor that Mr Carter had placed before it ... Mr Carter, Lord Carnarvon and his daughter certainly entered the Burial Chamber and the store chamber, which latter had no door, before the formal opening.' Later he wrote: 'The hole, unlike that in the outermost doorway, had not been closed and re-sealed by the cemetery officials, but by Mr Carter. Soon after I commenced work with Mr Carter he pointed out to me the closing and re-sealing, and when I said that it did not look like old work he admitted that it was not and that he had done it.'[22]

Before the official opening of the tomb, Lucas categorically remembered seeing, at Carter's house, a perfume box, which was subsequently found in the shrine. For those who had their suspicions regarding the activities of Carter and Carnarvon this was further confirmation that they had decided to conjure up some dramatic fairy tale describing their discovery of the tomb and to conceal their illicit first entry. The two partners in crime, however, seemed unperturbed by all the fuss. In December 1922, on his return to England, Carnarvon had an audience with George V at Buckingham Palace.

According to the court records, he assured the King that when they broke through the wall of the Burial Chamber, 'we will find five gilded shrines and the Little King will be inside when we dismantle them.'[25] How could Carnarvon know that the mummy would still be there, in its gilded shrine, if he had not been inside the Burial Chamber already?

The story of the discovery of Tutankhamun's tomb was now out and spreading unstoppably around the world. Rumours travelled through Egypt, further muddying the lines between fact and fantasy. One rumour was that locals had reported seeing three aeroplanes landing in the valley and leaving for unknown destinations, loaded with treasure. Carter acknowledged that he had heard these rumours but dismissed them as laughable. The general public, perhaps less cynical than they are today, were obviously happy to agree with him. No one wanted to be told that the two heroes, one a wealthy English aristocrat, the other a respected English academic, men of character who wore hats and suits and bow ties even in the most intense heat, would ever stoop to such depths as to steal the treasure they had discovered. Who was going to take the word of a few hysterical and uneducated 'natives' against the testimony of such fine men? Apparently no one.[24]

An official opening of the tomb was made on 29 November, the visitors, however, were only shown the Antechamber. The hole through to the Burial Chamber was strategically hidden with a basket and some reeds. The gathered company included provincial Egyptian personnel and personal friends such as Lady Newberry. According to T. G. H. James, in *Howard Carter: A Path to Tutankhamun*, a second viewing was arranged the following day when Pierre Lacau, Director-General of the Antiquities Service, Paul Tottenham, Adviser to the Ministry of Public Works and Sir Arthur Merton, representative from *The Times* newspaper were allowed to be present.[25] With the assistance of Carter, on 30 November news of the remarkable discovery was telegraphed all over the world.

Carter and Carnarvon had successfully managed to hide their deception. Yet all was not well within the Egyptian Antiquities Service. Lacau, together with his assistant, Tottenham, were not invited to the official opening and many Egyptian nationalists viewed this as a personal affront to their nation. For too long now, the British had plundered Egypt of its treasures. According to Nicholas Reeves in *The Complete Tutankhamun*, Arthur Mace, a conservation expert sent by the Metropolitan Museum, wrote from Luxor, 'Archaeology plus journalism is bad enough, but when you add politics it becomes a little too much.'[26] However, the sheer scale and drama of the tomb dwarfed all complaints about the high-handed manner in which the English archaeologists were behaving, and Carter and Carnarvon pushed on regardless. A list of dignitaries was assembled and invitations were sent out for the opening of the Burial Chamber on 17 February 1923.

On the day, Carter led the assembled crowd down the entrance steps and into the tomb. Carnarvon, following and in an exceptionally jovial mood, turned to the onlookers and joked, 'We're going to have a concert! Carter's going to sing us a song.' Hearing the quip, Arthur Weigall, one of the uninvited party standing around the entrance, retorted, 'If he goes down in that I give him six weeks to live.' It was to be a prophetic comment.[27]

Down beneath the ground Carter was, indeed, putting on a show. The Antechamber had been cleared and was set out with chairs for the audience to sit on. The hole that Carter and Carnarvon had made to get in and out of the Burial Chamber was now cleverly concealed by a small wooden platform. It was from here that

Carnarvon gave a short speech, thanking the workers and expressing his utmost gratitude to the Metropolitan Museum who had given so much assistance to the project. Then it was Carter's turn. With careful precision, he began to pick away at the plaster surrounding the Burial Chamber wall. He knew exactly what he would find but kept his audience riveted to their seats. Finally, when the hole was large enough, Carter peered through and said in a hushed voice, 'I see a wall of gold-blue faience.'[28]

For the gathered onlookers it was a magical moment and Carter was pretending to be as amazed as they were. As the hole became bigger the gleaming side of a golden shrine gradually became visible. Sliding inside the Chamber, and between the shrine walls, Carter continued to weave his magic by revealing a variety of wondrous objects including boxes, lamps and eleven magical oars. As documented by Thomas Hoving in *Tutankhamun: The Untold Story*, Carter then 'drew back the bolts of the outer shrine and opened the door, revealing a linen pall ... Behind this ancient piece of material lay the second shrine, the doors bolted and this time sealed ... That, Carter announced to the spellbound crowd, meant that they could be sure that grave robbers had not reached the body of the king.' No scriptwriter could have written a better series of cliff-hangers. A show as good as this was destined to run for ever.[29]

Carnarvon described his feelings that day to Arthur Merton of *The Times*.

I find it difficult to describe what I felt when I entered that inner chamber for, of a surety, I never dreamt I should gaze upon the amazing sight which met my eyes ... With the greatest care I followed Mr Carter in, and whatever emotion and excitement I may have felt when I entered the first chamber were as nothing when I was going into what undoubtedly was the practically untouched tomb of an Egyptian king. I have little doubt that as we remove shrine after shrine, the space between each succeeding set of walls will be found full of articles of the most intense interest, and judging from those already found probably of surpassing beauty. The work of dismantling will require the greatest care and dexterity and I anticipate constantly increasing interest as we go on, and quickening excitement until we reach the place where, I have no doubt, the body of the King lies undisturbed.[30]

Carter realized that he was going to need help in emptying the tomb and contacted Albert Lythgoe, Curator of the Metropolitan Museum's Egyptian Department, who had cabled to congratulate him and offer assistance. Carter cabled back. 'Thanks message [of congratulations]. Discovery colossal and need every assistance. Could you consider loan of Burton in recording in time being? Costs to us. Immediate reply would oblige. Every regards, Carter, Continental, Cairo.'

Lythgoe agreed immediately. It was in his interests to form the closest ties possible with Carter. He wanted to get first refusal for the Metropolitan on anything that might come to light. In the competitive world of the museums, Carter had become a good catch and Lythgoe's generosity was eventually rewarded handsomely.

Harry Burton was an Englishman who lived in Florence and had joined the Metropolitan in 1914. He had dug with Theodore Davis in the Valley of the Kings but was now attached to Carter as a photographer. The hundreds of glass negatives which he took over the following years of tomb clearance are among the best archaeological pictures ever taken. Other offers of help poured in and Carter was

The Tutankhamun Deception

able to put together a team of people he liked and trusted including Arthur Mace, Alfred Lucas, Pecky Callender, Percy Newberry (the man who first introduced Carter to Egyptology), Alan Gardiner, who was Carnarvon's friend and never really got on with Carter, James Breasted, Walter Hauser, Lindsley Foot Hall and Richard Adamson.

That is the official story of how Tutankhamun was discovered.

6

'Tut' Mania

*A story that opens like Aladdin's Cave and ends
like a Greek myth of Nemesis cannot fail to capture
the imagination of men and women...*[1]

Lady Burghclere

When Carter and Carnarvon staged the official opening of the Antechamber on 29 November 1922, they invited Arthur Merton, a friend of Carter's who was the local correspondent for *The Times* newspaper in London, and no other journalists. Merton played the story up for all it was worth. According to his report, this was 'the most sensational discovery of the century'.[2] The other papers of the world, particularly in London and Cairo, angered at having to read about such an immense story in a rival newspaper, nevertheless took up the story and ran with it. They had no option, it was too good for anyone to ignore. The media in the 1920s might not have been as instantaneous as it is today, relying as it did on the telegraph service, but it was still highly competitive and cut-throat. When editors had a story which they thought would run, they would play it up to the hilt. This one was due to run for years and everyone wanted a piece of it.[3]

Carter clearly found his sudden fame difficult to deal with. While

71

he doubtless liked the idea of being lauded by his peers, and probably saw his coveted knighthood coming a great deal closer, he did not relish the other side of his fame. In particular, he did not like having to deal with the public tramping all over his dig with their foolish and time-wasting questions. According to his colleague Arthur Mace, 'Carter's nerves are giving out with all the worry, and he'll have a breakdown if he isn't careful.'[4] Before 1922 the general public had never shown any particular interest in the finer points of archaeology which is, if you take out the treasure-hunting element, a fairly dry and esoteric subject for most people. But this discovery changed everything. Here was a story which any newspaper reader could understand and relate to: a boy pharaoh, entombed for 3,000 years, surrounded by limitless piles of gold bullion sculpted into the shape of fabulous works of art.

A description of the scene around the tomb published in the *Daily Telegraph* gives an idea of the pressure Carter was under.

The scene at the tomb awakened memories of Derby Day. The road leading to the rock-enclosed ravine ... was packed with vehicles and animals of every conceivable variety. The guides, donkey-boys, sellers of antiquities, and hawkers of lemonade were doing a roaring trade ... When the last article had been removed from the corridor today the newspaper correspondents began a spirited dash across the desert to the banks of the Nile upon donkeys, horses, camels and chariot-like sand-carts in a race to be the first to reach the telegraph offices.[5]

And still the world had yet to see what the actual coffins themselves would look like and to discover whether or not they held the mummy which the explorers so fervently hoped would be there.

America was reported to be 'obsessed' as everywhere you travelled, in the hotels, on the trains and so on, people were talking about the great Pharaoh and his treasures.[6] In the meantime and in the time-honoured tradition of their profession, journalists and commentators could speculate and exaggerate as much as they liked to make the story more attractive to their readers; and that they certainly did. The arid facts of history had suddenly come to life through the romantic personal story of a young boy king and his court. Then there were the tales of Carter and Carnarvon peering through a hole in the wall, and having the breath knocked from their bodies by the beauty of the secrets they had uncovered. The imagination of the whole world was working overtime.

Moreover, by telling the story about the hole in the blocked doorway so dramatically, and by building the suspense by pretending that they did not know what was behind the wall of the Ante-chamber that first day, Carter and Carnarvon had increased the potency of the myth a thousand times.

Like many a modern-day film or sports star suddenly catapulted into the limelight, Carter found that reporters were following him everywhere in the hope of uncovering a new angle on the story. Nor did a potential scoop necessarily have anything to do with the business of archaeology or ancient history. He was bombarded with letters and cables offering congratulations and assistance or begging for souvenirs. He might have been skilful at telling the story and building on the myth; he was not so adept at handling the resulting popularity.

The crowds besieging the tomb and lining the route to and from work each day became overwhelming. Many simply wanted to gaze at the events unfolding before their eyes so they could boast to their friends at home that they had been there. In addition, there were the so-called 'official' visitors who would just turn up uninvited, waving various permits from government ministers, interrupting the busy schedule and generally causing a nuisance. There were also the pressmen and hundreds of amateur photographers who would lean precariously over the tomb entrance attempting to secure the perfect picture to sell back home. Merton, of *The Times*, tried to deal with all the jostling and shouting crowds but, for one man alone, it was quite impossible. And, in the midst of all this madness, Carter was attempting to start the job of emptying the tomb. Under such hostile conditions the strain was beginning to tell. On 14 March a letter appeared in *The Times*, signed by the staff of the Metropolitan Museum of Art, Egypt Expedition, and by A. C. Mace as Associate Curator:

> The public should learn to curb its curiosity until the excavator sees fit to announce, at the time and in the manner he may choose, the result of his investigation ... Let us leave Mr Howard Carter and his assistants in peace to execute the task of preserving for us all these wonders, and let us respect their choice of the manner in which they choose to communicate to the public the result of their discoveries.'[7]

The declaration went by largely ignored. Those onlookers who were unable to get into the tomb would instead sit round the entrance, regardless of the heat, hindering Carter's workforce. It didn't help matters when Carter discovered that tourist agencies from all over the world were advertising 'trips to see the tomb.'[8] Life was becoming increasingly difficult, and for Carter it was his worst nightmare. The poorer the conditions became the more irritated he grew. He lost his temper frequently and refused to cooperate with the dozens of people who, each day, tried to take his picture on the way to or from work. Guests, many of them artists whose company Carter would normally have enjoyed, were ordered away. Whether he or Carnarvon would have staged their revelations differently if they had realized the consequences, we will never know, but it was the price they had to pay for their massive success.

'Tut Mania', as it was called, rapidly spread across Europe and America. In his book, *The Face of Tutankhamun*, Christopher Frayling states that, 'the craze touched every aspect of design, from the Tutankhamun Rag, played in the ballrooms of the finest hotels, to the latest lines in Egyptian-inspired garments, furniture, interior designs and fashion accessories.'[9] Throughout the 1920s the Western world was looking for a distraction from the world war it had just so recently endured. The discovery of the Tutankhamun tomb provided a frivolous diversion from reality. What greater escape could there be than to witness the fabulous wealth and efforts at immortality of an ancient and mysterious royal court which had been hidden for almost three thousand years?

Apart from the constant interruption by visitors, there were many stoppages to summon Mace and Lucas to the tomb to carry out emergency treatment before an object was removed, or to assist in the removal of an awkwardly placed piece.[10] However, all the pressure fell on Carter because he was the person actually on site working among the crowds. Carnarvon, although supportive to an extent, was used to the public attention, some would go as far as to say that he craved it, but Carter, struggling in the heat of the desert, was finding life exceptionally tiring. The immense job of removing, conserving and cataloguing each and every item from the tomb would eventually take him ten years.

Working with Carter was Burton, photographing generally and in detail at every stage of the clearance; Hauser and Hall, desperately trying to plot, plan and draw everything in situ while objects were being removed from beneath their drawing boards; and Lucas and Mace arriving with the paraffin wax to perform first aid on objects when needed.[11] No previous excavation in the Valley of the Kings had attempted such an exhaustive record of an archaeological find. It was painstaking, laborious work, which would have taxed the patience of any man, let alone the quick-tempered Carter. The tension was compounded by the conditions within the tomb itself: the airless heat increased by the electric lighting which had been installed to view the objects. Some of the confined spaces Carter and his colleagues had to work in for hours on end must have been excruciatingly painful for them. To the outside world it appeared that Carter had put together a well-oiled working team, but the cracks were beginning to show. In *Howard Carter Before Tutankhamun*, Reeves and Taylor quote a comment by Harry Burton, 'that man Carter is quite impossible!'[12] Under these conditions Carter must have been close to exploding, particularly as there were things that he very much wanted to keep away from prying eyes.

In order to keep the media at bay, Carter and Carnarvon hatched a plan which was eventually to make everything a hundred times more fraught. Today the exclusive newspaper deal is commonplace. Celebrities, or anyone who has been involved in a major news story, are routinely pressured by newspapers to sign exclusivity deals, guaranteeing not to talk to any of the opposition. Apart from the financial benefits offered, the newspapers usually promise to help protect the object of the news story from the unwelcome attentions of rival news organizations. The idea is that once the deal is signed, the opposition will realize they are beaten and go away. That is the theory, but in practice rival newspapers often look for ways to spoil the scoop by finding someone else to tell the same story or by simply making it up.

Carnarvon and Carter decided to do an exclusive deal with *The Times* of London, at the time the newspaper with the most substantial reputation world-wide, read by all the most influential people in Britain and those who ran the empire in other parts of the world. Carnarvon wrote to Carter on the subject:

> I am afraid that you have had a very poor time with the Press. I could have settled earlier, but I wanted to consult you and have your views ... I feel in this matter it would not do to, so to speak, auction the rights of journalistic publication, etc. I am afraid it would make the matter too common and commercial therefore I consider *The Times* offer the best thing that can be done. After all is said and done, it is the first paper in the world and even now has greater power and facilities than any other paper, which power I think very likely to increase under the new organisation and above all with Geoffrey Dawson, Editor. Even although I don't particularly care for him you are dealing with a straight gentleman.[13]

To Carnarvon *The Times* would have been the obvious choice, and for Carter there was the benefit of being able to work exclusively with Arthur Merton, a man he got on with and who didn't ask awkward questions. Carnarvon agreed an initial fee of £5,000 with the newspaper's editor, followed by a 75 per cent royalty on the subsequent sale of stories to other newspapers. At today's prices that is as substantial an offer as any modern newspaper would ever be able to offer.[14]

The justification which Carter and Carnarvon gave for striking the deal, which certainly had some truth in it, was that they couldn't spend all their time dealing with the swarms of journalists from Egypt and all over the world who were descending on the site, demanding tours, interviews and constant updates of what had been found. If *The Times* collected all the information and the rest bought it from them, that would cut down the pressure on Carter and his team as they worked. It seemed an eminently sensible suggestion to the two gentlemen who thought it up; to all the journalists – except Arthur Merton – it seemed outrageously elitist and arrogant. Uncharitable commentators suggested that the whole deal might simply be the result of Carnarvon's greed. The earl, who was also pursuing movie contracts in Hollywood, plus book and magazine deals with publishers, was doing this deal in order to make yet more money from the find, and treating the tomb as if it belonged to him personally and was on British soil.

While there are elements of truth in both interpretations of the motives for *The Times* deal, there was another even more pressing reason why Carter and Carnarvon wanted to keep tight control over media coverage of their affairs: they had a great deal to hide, and if they had allowed reporters in too often and too close, the journalists would have started putting two and two together and drawing some conclusions. As long as they could keep access to the tomb selective they stood a better chance of controlling the information that went out.

In his book *Tutankhamun: The Untold Story*, Hoving informs us that Arthur Merton was a personal friend of Carter's: someone who he could do business with, someone who would not rock the boat. Once *The Times* had an exclusive deal it was in Merton's interest to maintain the *status quo*. This was the biggest story in the world since the end of the war; *The Times* didn't want to do anything to play it down or cast doubt on the integrity of the heroes of the tale, not as long as it was able to sell the rights to the stories. It had become as much in *The Times*' interest as in Carter and Carnarvon's to keep alive the magic of the discovery in the minds of the reading public.[15]

Not surprisingly, the other newspapers, particularly the Egyptian ones who saw their country's ancient historical heritage monopolized by foreigners, were outraged. Egyptian nationalists were a growing force in the country and such undiplomatic behaviour on the part of the British infuriated them. For Egyptians to have to go to *The Times* to buy a story about their own heritage was adding insult to injury. Neither Carter nor Carnarvon could see what the fuss was all about. Weren't the British running Egypt? Hadn't they purchased the digging rights for the area? Hadn't they worked their fingers to the bone (well, Carter's fingers anyway) for ten years already, pouring their money (Carnarvon's that is) into one fruitless search after another? Weren't they providing much-needed employment to hundreds of local men and boys and bringing wealth into the country in the form of tourism? Weren't they helping the Egyptians to rediscover their past and preserve it in a way they were not able to do for themselves? Surely they were free to do whatever they wanted with 'their' tomb now that they had found it?

But it wasn't just the local press who were furious about the deal. Rivals in London and New York were equally incensed, particularly the *New York Times* and the *Daily Mail*. By excluding these papers, Carter and Carnarvon had made some of their most powerful enemies. Under the heading 'Tutankhamen Ltd' another London newspaper the *Daily Express* wrote in 1923:

While we have admiration for the faith and persistence which have brought so magnificent a reward to the labours of Lord Carnarvon, it is difficult to approve the manner in which he has seen fit to exploit his discovery ... the tomb is not his private property. He has not dug up the bones of his ancestors in the Welsh Mountains. He has stumbled upon a pharaoh in the land of the Egyptians ... and by making an exclusive secret of the contents of the inner tomb he has ranged against him the majority of the world's most influential newspapers.[16]

When Carnarvon's initial agreement with *The Times* expired, whether due to greed or perhaps arrogance, he immediately negotiated a second, albeit, it has to be said, for less money. Carter's friend, Arthur Merton, was appointed 'official spokesman for the dig' allowing him to update the members of the other papers. He wrote to Carter:

I beg to confirm my acceptance of your offer to join your staff in the capacity of publicity agent. As agreed between us, I shall represent you in the Valley of the Kings in all publicity matters connected with the work at the tomb of Tutankhamun, and, as regards the publication of news and data, I shall only communicate such information as you may consent to publish, to such quarters as you may, from time to time, indicate to me.[17]

Not surprisingly, this aggravated the situation even further.

On 24 December 1922, Carnarvon wrote to Carter informing him about the most lucrative way to sell the story to the media. He had decided, he said, to sell the film rights to Goldwyn Ltd in Hollywood for the making of a spectacular movie. This was the golden age of Hollywood, and what better subject could there be than the majestic Valley of the Kings, a spectacular pile of treasures and two intrepid heroes battling against the elements to discover the truth. The earl threw himself wholeheartedly into both the creative and business sides of the project. The press became even more vociferous in their condemnation. Carter and Carnarvon were making enemies in every direction, but this didn't bother Carnarvon. The press could be as poisonous towards him as they liked; when you were as rich and as aristocratic as he was it was water off a duck's back. If anyone pointed out what the journalists were saying he would shrug it off. Surely, he reasoned charmingly, no one took what they read in the newspapers seriously.

And then, just when it seemed the press coverage could not get any worse, the media got hold of the story of 'the curse'.

7

THE MUMMY'S CURSE

... all sane people should dismiss such inventions with contempt.[1]
Howard Carter

Quite where the rumours of the curse started is unclear. What is certain is that by scoffing at them in the media, Carter drew attention to them, gave them greater credence and spread them still further. If there was something to deny, the public reasoned, then the principle of 'no smoke without fire' must apply.

In the end, the curse became almost as big a story as the original tale of the boy king and the discovery of the tomb. The mummy, rising from the dead, ragged, rotting bandages unravelling as he (or she) lurched ominously and unstoppably down upon a helpless heroine, became as much of a cliché in the horror genre as vampires like Count Dracula and man-made monsters from Doctor Franken-stein's laboratory. The Egyptian mummy took its place alongside Jekyll and Hyde, Jack the Ripper and voodoo zombies in the inter-national pantheon of horror icons.

According to the press, the first human victim of the curse was Carnarvon himself, on 2 April 1923, just four months after the dramatic announcement of the discovery of the tomb. The official story was that he had been bitten by a mosquito on the cheek while taking a few days' rest after the opening of the Burial Chamber. By shaving the bite he infected it and before long a fever had set in. Already in weak health and further exhausted by the strenuous last few months, the fifty-seven-year-old earl was put to bed by his devoted daughter, Evelyn. He seemed to recover after a couple of days and even talked of returning to the tomb. However, a relapse put him back into bed and Evelyn made arrangements for him to be moved to the Continental-Savoy in Cairo. But he grew worse and contracted pneumonia, which eventually carried him off.

The Egyptologist Alan Gardiner recorded in his book, *My Working Years*:

It was the culmination of a season of both excitement and sorrows. He [Carnarvon] might, perhaps, have recovered from the mosquito bite which he got in Luxor if he had taken better care of himself . . . He came down to Cairo and invited me to dine with him at the Mohammed Ali Club. He expressed himself very tired and despondent but insisted on going to see a film. There he said that his face was hurting and I begged him to go back to the hotel, the Continental. But no, he would see the film to the finish, and he would never go out of doors again despite the presence of the best doctors in Cairo.[2]

The death of Lord Carnarvon in Cairo, watched over by Almina, Evelyn and his son Lord Porchester, who had been called from army service in India, brought forth reports of strange events. The first of those was reported by the *Daily Express* on 6 April 1923. The journalist claimed that, as Carnarvon drew his last breath, 'suddenly all the lights in Cairo Hospital went out leaving them all in complete darkness. After a lapse of a few minutes the lights came on again, only to go out abruptly. This curious occurrence was interpreted by those anxiously awaiting news as an omen of evil.'[3]

Over the next few weeks the 'lights' story began to develop. According to reports it wasn't just the lights in Cairo that had gone out, in fact, the entire electricity supply of the city, four entire grids, failed for a full five minutes at the exact time of Carnarvon's death. Lord Allenby himself confirmed the Cairo blackout. He is said to have asked the engineer in charge of the electricity supply for an explanation, but none was forthcoming. 'The Curse of the Pharaoh' and 'The Curse of the King' were about to become the new, repetitive headline.[4]

On 24 March 1923 the *Daily Express* reprinted a letter to the *New York World* in which the veteran novelist Marie Corelli remarked that she had warned Carnarvon of his fate. Under the dramatic heading, 'Pharaohs Guarded by Poisons? Lord Carnarvon Warned By Marie Corelli', she said that she had seen the hand of the pharaoh rather than the bite of the mosquito in his lordship's illness, even before he died, and had written to him, expressing the wish that nothing unfortunate would happen to him in the pursuit of his discoveries. 'I cannot but think,' Corelli wrote, 'that some risks are run by breaking into the last rest of the King of Egypt whose tomb is specially and solemnly guarded, and robbing him of his possessions.'[5]

Contrary to popular opinion, Egyptian tomb curses or booby traps are rare. In considering the activities of tomb-robbers, it was the complex design of the tomb, and their associated defence mechanisms that would deter the would-be burglar rather than dark supernatural forces. For example, during the Twelfth and Thirteenth Dynasties, certain coffins from wealthy burials were equipped with a special locking mechanism to prevent them being reopened.[6] There are a few documented examples of curses, dating to the Old and Middle Kingdoms respectively, yet considering that the vast majority of ancient Egyptian tombs have been plundered in antiquity, such curses were obviously not effective.

A well known clairvoyant, Count Louis Harmon, known as Cheiro, made a similar revelation in his book *Real Life Stories* (1934). An ancient Egyptian sorceress, 'the seventh daughter of the King Atennaten', Princess Mekitaten, had apparently been kind enough to transmit the warning to him through a kind of automatic writing. 'It was to the effect that on his arrival at the tomb of Tut-Ankh-Amen [Lord Carnarvon] was not to allow any of the relics found in it to be removed or taken away.' The message concluded by saying that if he disobeyed the warning he would suffer an injury while in the tomb, a sickness from which he would never recover, and that 'death would claim him in Egypt'.[7]

To counteract the daily press speculation that Carnarvon was intending to remove the King's mummy and transport him back to England, he wrote in *The Times* on 24 February 1923:

At the present moment, King Tutankhamun rests, to the best of our belief, where he was originally placed. When the time comes to ascertain whether it *is* the mummy of the king, I personally, and those associated with me, are most anxious that arrangement should be made to leave his body in the sarcophagus in its present resting place ... I may say that I have not yet discussed the point, nor do I view with favour the somewhat unwholesome and morbid taste which some people seem to enjoy by looking at mummies exposed in glass cases in museums.[8]

It is hard to see why it is any more 'unwholesome and morbid' to want to look at mummies in glass cases than to dig them up in the first place, but the earl was making a point. There was a strong body of opinion which felt that perhaps no one, not even an English earl, had the right to dig up people who had clearly expressed a desire to be left in peace throughout eternity. Earlier that same month, at the height of the rumours in the press, a correspondent to *The Times* had made the same point through a disquieting comparison between the corpse of the pharaoh and that of the late Queen Victoria herself.

I wonder how many of us, born and brought up in the Victorian era, would like to think that in the year, say, 5923, the tomb of Queen Victoria would be invaded by a party of foreigners who robbed it of its contents, took the body of the great Queen from the mausoleum in which it had been placed amid the grief of the whole people, and exhibited it to all and sundry who might wish to see it. The question arises whether such treatment as we should count unseemly in the case of the great English Queen, is not equally unseemly in the case of King Tutankhamun.[9]

It is a point that is hard to dispute ethically and morally. But the excitement of the discovery was irresistible to everyone. There was no place for moral qualms when the whole world was holding its breath.

Furthermore, the rumours about curses refused to abate, adding a *frisson* of danger to the already heady mixture of adventure and mystery which the watching world was enjoying and brushing aside awkward scruples over disturbing the corpse.

Another wild press story involved the so-called 'clay tablet' said to have been found over the entrance of the tomb. Documented by Frayling in *The Face of Tutankhamun*, it was allegedly removed and catalogued by Carter and then erased from the written record and buried in the sand, because the excavators were 'worried that the Egyptian labourers would take it seriously and the work schedule would be disrupted.'[10] The opening lines on the tablet supposedly read: 'As to anyone who violates my body which is in the tomb and who shall remove my image from my tomb, he shall be hateful to the gods, and he shall not receive water on the altar of Osiris, neither shall he bequeath his property to his children for ever and ever.'[11] This was duly fine-tuned to read, 'Death shall come on swift wings to whoever toucheth the tomb of the Pharaoh.'[12] There is no evidence whatsoever that the clay tablet existed.

Carter, it would appear, subscribed to neither train of thought. Or so you would think. In his book, *The Tomb of Tut-Ankh-Amen* he said:

It has been stated in various quarters that there are actual physical dangers hidden in Tutankhamun's tomb – mysterious forces, called into being by some malefic power, to take vengeance on whomsoever should dare to pass its portals. There was perhaps no place in the world freer from risks than the tomb ... Unpardonable and mendacious statements of this nature have been published and repeated in various quarters with a sort of malicious satisfaction. It is indeed difficult to speak of this form of 'ghostly' calumny with calm. If it be not actually libellous, it points in that spiteful direction, and all sane people should dismiss such inventions with contempt.'[13]

On 4 October 1924 Carter was quoted as saying he had not the slightest belief that any occult influence was responsible for Carnarvon's death and that he had no fears for himself in that direction. 'It is rather too much too ask me to believe that some spook is keeping watch and ward over the dead Pharaoh, ready to wreck vengeance on anyone who goes too near.'[14]

However, it appears that even Carter, in his early years when working in the Valley of the Kings seems to have romanced about the existence of 'the curse of the pharaohs'. In his book *Howard Carter: The Path To Tutankhamun*, T. G. H. James recollects that when showing a young female visitor round the newly unearthed tomb of Amenophis II, Carter was quoted as saying, 'The pharaoh's mummy was probably protected ... by a curse pronounced in the band of hieroglyphics around the top of the sarcophagus upon any marauding hands.'[15] In addition he apparently once told a New York *Time* reporter about 'a novel of travel which some literary man of the time had written to entertain Tutankhamun on his pilgrimage throughout the lower world.'[16] No such novel has ever been found and there is no evidence of a curse upon the sarcophagus.

Just six weeks before he died, Carnarvon attended the official opening of the Burial Chamber within the tomb. Arthur Weigall, excluded from the invitation list and having to watch the arrival of the VIPs from beside the entrance rather as the crowds now watch the film stars arriving on Oscar night, made his comment about Carnarvon being dead in six weeks if he went into the tomb in the flippant mood he was exhibiting. Weigall was now a special correspondent for the *Daily Mail*, one of the newspapers which felt most aggrieved by the *Times* deal. He later admitted that he had made the remark but could give no explanation for why he might have done so, apart from being annoyed by the earl's manner. He certainly couldn't explain how he had come to predict the time of Carnarvon's death so accurately.

The Mummy's Curse

Once the idea of the curse had taken root in the popular imagination it spread like a malignant cancer. Reports appeared of an inscription in the tomb which read, 'Death shall come on swift wings to him that toucheth the tomb of Pharaoh,' and people suddenly remembered the story of Carter's canary. In an attempt to brighten up his modest accommodation, Carter had bought a canary in a cage just before the final dig. On the day the tomb was opened a cobra was said to have entered his rooms and swallowed the little songbird. The event was deemed extraordinary and significant for two reasons: firstly the cobra was an extremely rare sight in the area and secondly it was a symbolic serpent which the pharaohs often had carved on the brows of their headdresses to ward off their enemies. The conclusion which many people jumped to, therefore, was that the snake had been sent by the dead pharaoh as a warning to Carter not to trespass any further.[17]

Herbert Winlock described in a letter the effect the incident had on the workers:

When Carter came out last October, alone, he got a canary bird, in Cairo, in a gilded cage to cheer up what he figured was going to be a lonely and deserted house. Carter, coming over to his house with his servant, Abdul Ali, carrying the canary behind him and the guards and the foremen greeting him and right off, when they see a golden bird they say: '*Mabrook* – it's a bird of gold that will bring luck. This year we will find *inshallah* (God willing) a tomb full of gold.' Within a week they had made the most fabulous find of all time and at first the tomb was called 'the tomb of the Golden Bird' by the natives. The canary almost had a halo around its cage.

As soon as he struck the tomb, Carter got Callender from

Erment and shortly afterwards Carnarvon arrived and Carter went to Cairo to meet him. Callender was living alone in Carter's house with the bird consigned to his especial care. Suddenly, one afternoon he heard a fluttering and squeaking and went into the next room and there in the cage with the bird was a cobra just in the act of gulping the canary down, halo and all.

Now, cobras had never been known around there before, and cobras, as every native knew, grow on the heads of Old Kings. The conclusion was obvious. The King's serpent had struck at the mascot who had given away the secret of the tomb. And the sequel was equally obvious – at least to them, though I admit to have lost some links in the chain of argument – that before the winter was out someone would die. It was all very dismal.[18]

The canary was not the only pet to be struck down by the 'curse'. A thousand miles away at Highclere Castle, the earl's dog, a terrier named Susie, who, according to the staff pined for Carnarvon during his absence in Egypt, is reputed to have howled inconsolably and died within minutes of the earl.[19]

There were also a number of high-profile deaths among those who knew what Carter and Carnarvon had been up to and these may have been connected, if not by an ancient curse, perhaps by a contemporary one. Documented by Frayling in *The Face of Tutankhamun*, they form an impressive list. Carnarvon's younger half-brother, Aubrey Herbert, died six months after him. Carter's secretary, Richard Bethel, was found dead in strange circumstances at his club about six years later and Bethel's father, Lord Westbury, died in very suspicious circumstances a short time after. An eight-year-old child was then killed by Lord Westbury's hearse. An X-ray specialist died *en route* to examine the mummy and a railroad magnate called George Jay Gould died of pneumonia after visiting the tomb. An Egyptian, Prince Ali Fahmy Bey, was shot by his wife at the Savoy Hotel in London after viewing the tomb. Carter's assistant, Arthur Mace, the Metropolitan Museum's conservationist, died before the work of clearing had been completed. A French Egyptologist fell to his death after viewing the tomb and a manual attendant at the British Museum dropped dead while labelling some objects from the tomb. A lecturer in archaeology from Leeds and Arthur Weigall, the Egyptologist, both died younger than might have been expected.[20]

Professional Egyptologists refused, like Carter, to believe in the curse. According to a newspaper report, Herbert Winlock, Director of the Metropolitan Museum, compiled a dossier illustrating the gibberish surrounding the extraordinary number of deaths associated with the tomb. He insisted that no objects from the tomb were present in the collection of Egyptian Antiquities in the British Museum when its curator at the time died. He also argued that although Arthur Weigall had been closely associated with Carter's and Carnarvon's 'coming and goings' in the Valley of the Kings for years, much to his own disgust, he was not allowed into the tomb except as a tourist. 'If tourists are subject to the curse,' Winlock wrote, 'it should be remembered that a large number of them are elderly people travelling to Egypt for their health.' In addition, he pointed out that the expedition's conservator, Arthur Mace, was in exceptional bad health with heart, chest and stomach problems exacerbated by several years of 'breathing cloth dust in confined spaces', and subsequently died of pleurisy and pneumonia. The chart then illustrated that of the twenty-six people, who were there when the tomb was opened, twenty were still in sound health.[21]

The rumours continued nonetheless with rival newspapers now fighting to promote their own version of the story. On the same day the *Daily Express* ran the piece about the lights going out in Cairo at the moment that Carnarvon died, the *Daily Mail* printed an article about a dreaded mosquito which 'may have previously settled on embalming fluid found buried with Tutankhamun.'[22] To this, Carter's friend and mentor, Professor Percy Newberry, replied, 'In the valley itself there are no mosquitoes, so the poisonous bite must have occurred in Luxor.'[23] No doubt Carter thought the story he and Carnarvon had been telling was dramatic enough without these unwelcome attentions. In later life he became blunter in his ripostes to anyone who raised the subject: 'The answer is spherical and in the plural ... And as a matter of fact the word "Osiris" referred to the deceased. And by the way, I am still alive.'[24] 'If there was any curse,' he wrote, 'it took the form of Messrs Creepy, Crawly Biteum and Co.' – the company of nasty insects which bit him when he was camping out in the desert.'[25]

Carnarvon was buried at Highclere Castle on 28 April 1923 at the vantage point of his choice, where he could keep an eternal eye on his stud farms, his gardens and the lakes and lawns, reaching as far as the eye could see.[26] Only six weeks after the official opening of the tomb, Carter had lost his most trusted friend and ally. If there was any real curse it was the legacy of Carnarvon's death for Carter. With Carnarvon alive there had been a chance that the emerging conflicts between the discoverers of the tomb and their many enemies within the press and the Egyptian authorities could have been resolved; when necessary, Carnarvon knew how to turn on the aristocratic charm and get his way. Things, in the hands of the ill-tempered Carter, would go from bad to worse.

8

THE TRUE STORY OF
DISCOVERY AND ROBBERY

Sometimes when I have been sitting at work alone ... [in a tomb in
the Valley of the Kings] I have been oppressed by the silence and the
mystery ... and if, after this lapse of three thousand years, one is still
conscious of the awful sanctity ... one wonders what must have been
the sensations of the ancient thieves who penetrated by the light of
a flickering oil lamp into the very presence of the dead.[1]

Arthur Weigall

All that you have read so far is the truth as it has been accepted,
with some adaptations by different scholars and experts to try to
explain various anomalies, about how Carter and Carnarvon found
and emptied the tomb of Tutankhamun.

It is nothing but half truths and lies.

I will now explain what I think actually happened. It is an infinitely
more shocking tale of robbery and murder than has been told until
now, and does not rely on the existence of any trumped-up 'mummy's
curse'. I believe that Howard Carter and Lord Carnarvon conned the
whole world and that in the course of executing their trick (which
made them fabulously rich) they unearthed a secret so potentially
damaging to world order that a string of murders were instigated to
ensure that the truth never saw the light of day.

To examine this bold assertion, we will re-examine the story from the beginning to see what really happened.

Carter was a systematic and methodical man: his methods of searching and excavation were highly precise. He was also a man with an enormous amount to prove to the world. Like many of us he liked the idea of becoming wealthy, but he was also driven by a fierce desire for social respectability and more; he yearned for a knighthood, or possibly even a peerage. There must have been times when he was visiting Carnarvon at the beautiful Highclere Castle estate when he fantasized about one day being elevated to a similar level himself. He took on his friend's mannerisms and style of dress; portraits of Carter (particularly one by his brother) in the latter part of his life show a man who looks every bit as much of a gentleman as his partner. When he was sacked from the Antiquities Service and had to earn his living as best he could amongst the tourists and tomb robbers, Carter's resolve to show the world that they were wrong about him can only have strengthened.

I believe that by the time he was sacked he already knew where the tomb of Tutankhamun was, having been shown a way in through passages from other tombs by the El-Rassul, and simply needed the opportunity, and the money, to exploit it. He could have gone into the tomb with the El-Rassul and lived off the proceeds of whatever they could carry out and sell, but that wouldn't have given him the respectability which he craved. Being a successful tomb robber might provide him with the wealth he needed, but it would never gain him a knighthood and world acclaim.

When he was introduced to Carnarvon, Carter saw his opportunity. The earl had money, status and shared many of Carter's ambitions if for different reasons. Running an estate the size of Highclere on inherited money must have been a considerable burden, even for a man with such an enormous inheritance. Carnarvon had also been in the shadow of his statesman father and the years in which he was going to be able to prove himself were running out. By joining forces with Carter, Carnarvon could make his own mark, possibly even outshine his father and secure the future of the family estate.

Then Theodore Davis stepped in and took the concession for the area that Carter already knew held the tomb that they so wanted to uncover. Ever since he had deliberately sabotaged his own career as an inspector in order to pursue his freelance activities, Carter had been waiting for this moment. Now, because of Davis, he was going to have to wait a bit longer. So, while Davis dug around the valley in his own haphazard and amateurish manner, Carter and Carnarvon had to content themselves with working in other places, while keeping a careful eye on what Davis was up to and hoping that he would not accidentally stumble on the prize which they believed should be theirs.

It was Carter who advised Davis to give up digging for fear that he would undermine the road, when the American was just a few feet away from the walls of the tomb. I am certain that Carter already knew how close Davis was to the treasure; if he did not, then it was the most extraordinary coincidence. I believe that he and Carnarvon and the El-Rassul were already hard at work inside the tomb of Tutankhamun and, had Davis suddenly broken in and come upon them, they would have been exposed for the robbers they actually were.

In 1908 Davis did find a tomb containing pieces stamped with Tutankhamun's name and that of his wife, Ankhesenpaaten, plus a small alabaster statue and some gold foil showing the young king hunting on his chariot. Davis was so sure he had found the last resting place of Tutankhamun that he co-authored a book with Maspero, Daressy and Crane, all respected Egyptologists, entitled *The Tombs of Harmhabi and Tutankhamun.* He was absolutely correct; he had discovered part of Tutankhamun's tomb. So, if disaster was to be averted, Carter had to persuade him that there was nothing else to be found.

Carter declared that Davis was mistaken. He said the tomb was too small to be that of a king and in this he was right. What Davis had in fact found was a connecting passage to Tutankhamun's tomb. Only Carter knew where the pharaoh was and he had no intention of telling Davis, or the rest of the world, until he was in complete possession and ready to present it as a spectacular piece of theatre. After years of working in the valley, Carter knew that the tombs of the Eighteenth Dynasty rulers were interconnected and that Tutankhamun's final resting place lay under that of Ramesses VI. It was also connected to KV5 – the tombs were designated by finders to make identification simple, KV5 thus becomes Kings Valley, Tomb 5 – and to the cache that Davis had discovered.

Once Carter had found the entrance used by the priests some 3,000 years before, he had to make absolutely certain that no one got in before him. He was no longer in a position of authority so he couldn't cancel Davis's concession nor could he disclose what he had discovered. He simply had to bide his time until an opportunity presented itself. No wonder he watched like a hawk every move that Davis made. As soon as Davis had given up – encouraged by Carter and Carnarvon to do so – the two friends pounced on the concession and began to work.

In 1909 Davis had given the artefacts he had discovered with Ayrton, his archaeologist after Carter, to Herbert Winlock, who later became director of the Metropolitan Museum, to ship to New York.

They were then forgotten until 1921, when Winlock decided to examine them more carefully. To his amazement, he discovered that not only did the jugs, the clay items and some of the seals bear the seal of Tutankhamun, they also carried the seal of the royal necropolis. This was proof positive that the boy king had been interred in the valley.[2]

Winlock was close to Carter and, thinking that it would help his friend immensely in his quest for the tomb, lost no time in telling him. But by then Carter already knew; the information Winlock gave him merely confirmed to everyone else that Carter was on to something. But with more attention focused on what they were doing, Carter and Carnarvon had to be more cautious in their activities. The time was drawing near when they would have to stop secretly removing items, announce they had located the tomb and find a convincing way to cover up what they had been up to.

To the outside world Carter still appeared to be searching on the surface of the Valley of the Kings for the entrance to the tomb, and in a way he was: he still did not know exactly where the tomb lay in relation to all the others. By the time Maspero gave Carter and Carnarvon their licence, Carter had already narrowed his search down to a few thousand square yards, although he pretended he had not. He was also already secretly working inside the tomb, but he needed to calculate its exact position in relation to the surface, because he was going to need to find a position from which he could create a false entrance to cover up the work which had been going on below ground for some years. In his notes on the excavation work he wrote, 'the difficulty was to know where to begin for mountains of rubbish encumbered the ground in all directions, and no sort of record had ever been kept as to which areas had been properly excavated and which had not.'[3] This was patently not true.

According to Thomas Hoving in *Tutankhamun: The Untold Story*, Charles Wilkinson of the Metropolitan Museum later said that Carter knew exactly where the earlier excavators had explored and had a pretty good idea of what was still virgin territory.[4]

Of course Carter could locate the tomb: he had already discovered it with the El-Rassul family, the most experienced tomb robbers in all Egypt. He was also in a position to empty it, using their army of workers, knowing that he could rely on their absolute discretion, and at the same time create a smokescreen by doing other archaeological work in different places to confuse the authorities and blind rival archaeologists. Carter and Carnarvon needed to buy time, time in which they could take what they wanted from the tombs and prepare what was left for the official discovery which would make their reputations and provide authenticity, fame and value to all the artefacts which they were collecting.

In his search for the perfect fake entrance site, Carter decided to concentrate on digging down to the bedrock in the small triangular plot of land between the tombs of Ramesses VI, Ramesses II and Merenptah, insisting that this be the area of search. He had devised a grid system, which he had learned from the army, to help him work out exactly how the tombs lay in relation to one another. Something much like a grid was laid out and Carter systematically worked his way through the squares until he was certain he had the correct location and configuration of the burial site. A writer called Jon Manchip White tells a story, which he in turn was told by an aged resident of Luxor, about a British soldier during World War I who purchased a roll of papyrus from an Egyptian farmer, who had found it accidentally. The soldier couldn't read the roll which later came into the hands of Carter, who could. According to Manchip White's informant, who was thirteen at the time of the story, the papyrus pinpointed the location of Tutankhamun's tomb and even listed its contents. Carter decided, apparently, to keep this knowledge to himself and to concentrate his search around the tomb of Ramesses VI.[5]

Carnarvon was happy to go along with Carter's suggestions, confident that his partner was arranging things to their best possible advantage, and content with the artefacts secretly being extracted from the tomb and shipped to him.

This story, however, is pure hearsay and it is much more likely that Carter found the tomb through the El-Rassul.

Carter cleared the area down to the foot of Ramesses' tomb. In so doing he came across the site of the workmen's huts which had been built, in antiquity, over a group of boulders. This, he must have decided, would be the perfect location for the false entrance to the tomb. He then shifted his workforce away from the boulders and began clearing in the opposite direction. Why he should do this was never officially explained since the presence of boulders often indicates a nearby tomb. When questioned later about this sudden change in direction, Carter gave the rather lame excuse that tourists would shortly be arriving for the season and his excavations would hinder their access to the tomb of Ramesses VI.

It is more likely that the prospect of large crowds milling around him while he worked prompted him to move in the other direction. As we have seen, he disliked crowds intensely and he would be unable to work in peace on the construction of a false entrance if he was constantly being watched. He needed to buy more time and to distract attention from the site where he needed to do his preparatory work. At this stage he was in no hurry. All he was doing on the surface of the valley was mapping out the whole area according to the grid in order to ascertain the exact parameters of the tomb. He had to be absolutely certain where the tomb of the young monarch was positioned in relation to nearby tombs, especially that of Ramesses VI, so that he could finalize his plans for the discovery. To rush things now would have been ridiculous after so many years of profitable preparation.

Carter, the lone European on the site for much of the time, had to contend with the stifling heat, the workers underfoot, the dirt and choking dust everywhere. Little wonder he was becoming more and more peevish, moody and irascible.

Although the personal loyalty of his gang to him was never in question, their natural instincts were. Carter had to be certain all the time that none of them were slipping any choice little pieces out into the marketplace ahead of his own timetable. For any of the multitude of objects that had been removed before the official discovery to surface before the opening of the tomb would be a disaster of the highest magnitude. Any of the workers secreting an object, no matter how small, and later selling it on the black market could give everything away.

All the time he was at work on the surface, his friends, the El-Rassul, were working away below the surface removing treasure of incalculable value. This clandestine operation continued for years with World War I providing the perfect cover for their activities. The attention of the press and the protectorate authorities was distracted by more serious matters than archaeology, and although Carter was occupied from time to time with the war effort, in effect he had four years in which to work with the spotlight of international attention focused elsewhere.

It is my belief that Carter discovered the tomb almost immediately after he restarted digging in 1914, nearly eight years before the 'official' discovery on that November night in 1922. Reading their descriptions of their feelings at the staged discovery eight years later, we can only imagine how Carter and Carnarvon must have felt as they truly came through into the tomb for the first time and realized that they had stumbled on what must have been the biggest cache of gold and jewels in existence. They must have been painfully torn between an urge to shout their find to the world and bask in the glory, and a realization that if they could keep the secret for a few years they could ensure that the bulk of the treasure went to them. To maintain that secret for eight years, as they worked to clear the tombs and reconstruct history, was a tremendous feat of self-control and man management. The fact that they got away with it is extraordinary, but with the benefit of hindsight, it is possible to see exactly how they did it.

There are several pieces of evidence that suggest they were in the tombs years before they announced the discovery. The most compelling is a ring given by Carnarvon to Edward Harkness, the Chairman of the Board of the Metropolitan Museum, in 1921. The ring, which bore the cartouche of Tutankhamun, was known to have been in circulation for seven years by that stage. It could only have come from the young king's tomb.

What Carter and Carnarvon had actually discovered was a tomb far bigger than the one that the public would later be led to believe housed Tutankhamun. They then systematically robbed it of around four fifths of its wealth between 1914 and 1922, still leaving enough treasure to amaze the world when they finally simulated the discovery.

Over the years, every story that they put out was carefully planned to muddy the waters and confuse the experts. There was the rumour, for instance, which they circulated about Carnarvon being about to give up the search in 1922 and Carter offering to pay for it himself, so impressing the earl that he insisted on financing it after all. It seems highly unlikely that this is true when seen in the context of all the other evidence. Both of them knew that this would be the last season of 'searching' because they had decided that now was the time to stage the discovery. They merely wanted to reinforce in the public mind the idea that even they had begun to suspect that it was all a wild-goose chase.

My suspicions were first aroused when I visited the Cairo museum and saw the size of the Tutankhamun display there. I had already been to the empty tomb where the boy's mummy still lies, and I could not imagine how the immense treasure which I saw laid out before me in the museum could all have come from those few small rooms. Then, as I investigated further, I discovered that there are displays of artefacts from the tomb in thirteen other museums around the world, including the British Museum, and that excludes the material that must be in the hands of private collectors or has disappeared altogether. If you put together all these fabulous items it becomes impossible to believe that they could all have come from the chambers that thousands of tourists visit every year, marvelling at how cramped they are for the tremendous work that was carried out there. There was just too much. It is like trying to convince us that all the contents of Buckingham Palace were discovered in Anne Hathaway's cottage.

By stressing how everything was stacked chaotically into the Antechamber, Annexe and Treasury areas, Carter and Carnarvon managed to confuse the picture and make it impossible for anyone other than those who were actually working on the clearance to work out exactly what was and wasn't there. If you go into the attic or cellar of any old family house and look at the way discarded furniture, trunks and bric-a-brac have built up over the years, you can picture what it must have looked like when the chambers were first opened to the public. How could anyone have gained any accurate idea of exactly what was there?

When I went back to the tomb to have a second look I was struck by a number of other inconsistencies. If this pharaoh merited such a treasure trove of worldly goods to see him through eternity, why was he housed in such meagre accommodation? There was the possible explanation that he had died unexpectedly young and the preparations simply hadn't been made in time, but the degree of wealth buried with him suggested that was not the case. If they had had time to put together such an immense collection, wouldn't they have had time to build a tomb large enough to house it in some order and dignity? Above all else, why was the entrance to the tomb so small that the priests had actually cut the axles of the six chariots in half in order to get them through the doorway? How difficult would it have been for them to make the entrance a few metres wider? An extra week's work perhaps? Even if they had had to take the chariots to pieces in order to get them through the entrance, would they not have put them back together again once they were inside?

We are talking about priests and servants who were willing to go to enormous lengths to bury their kings in a fitting manner. Was it really likely that they would chop up the chariots just to get them through a small doorway and then leave them propped up against one another in disarray? What use would they be to the young king like that? How would they have drawn him through the underworld in pieces?

For many years I thought about the subject and read everything I could find – official versions from Carter and his team and unofficial versions from their critics – and slowly the possibility dawned on me that the entire discovery had been stage-managed. The entrance, which was supposed to have been discovered by the water boy was not actually the official entrance at all. It was the exit which Carter and Carnarvon had created in order to get in and out of the tomb once they had sealed the real entrance up. I discovered that Carter had actually changed his story about the water boy and the hidden step several times. When he was touring America, towards the end of his career, Carter told Lee Keedick, the organizer of the tour, that, contrary to what he wrote in the book, 'the step had been found a bit outside the area that he had instructed his foreman to begin with the previous evening'.[6]

The fabrication about the water boy was necessary to establish that the uncovered steps to the tomb be reported as covered. That way Carter could dig them out as far as the first sealed door, partially excavate this and then fill it all in, ostensibly to wait for the arrival of his patron and friend, Carnarvon. The reason for not uncovering the whole door on that first night was that he needed to devote the remaining hours of light to refilling the part he had cleared. In reality, since he hadn't dug it out in the first place, what he did was simply to fill it in with the seals on the so-called doorways in place. He didn't need to dig it out because he knew the entrance was there. He knew that because he had built it himself.

The moment I started to doubt the water boy story it suddenly seemed so incredibly flimsy that I couldn't understand how I, and the rest of the world, had believed it for so long. No one ever met this mythical boy except Carter. Everyone simply took his word for the boy's existence because it is another piece in the perfect fairy tale. A small, penniless, ignorant boy, armed with nothing but a stick, unearths an entrance which has been defeating the finest and most educated minds in the world for hundreds of years. It's irresistible. It's story-telling at its finest and most magical.

If he was such a lowly, ignorant boy, however, how would he know to cover his find up so that 'other archaeologists' wouldn't see it? How would he know one archaeologist from another? How would he know that Carter was the man to go to? How would he possibly be aware that a hard surface beneath the sand was so significant? The whole area is a mass of rock and the steps were found beneath the old workmen's huts, where hard surfaces must have abounded. What made this small boy believe that he had found something so much more important than everything else that was being unearthed and moved about in the valley by the army of workers?

Suddenly it was blindingly clear to me that Carter had invented the story. So, if he had invented that, had he invented everything else?

When I looked a little further into it, I discovered that by the date when Carnarvon was supposed to have received the telegram from Carter telling him to come quickly because he had made an interesting find, Carnarvon had already lavishly stocked the larder at the excavation. Would he have done that unless he had known that he was about to be summoned to the site? Of course not. He wanted everything to be ready for his arrival so that he would be able to celebrate the discovery of a tomb – which had not yet been officially found – in his usual grand style. When Carter arrived in the valley for the final act of the search he brought with him a vast amount of provisions of the highest standard, including the finest wines available, which Carnarvon had had shipped out from Fortnum and Mason, the famous Piccadilly grocer's shop for the moneyed classes.[7] It seems clear that Carnarvon knew exactly when he would receive the call to come out for the opening of the tomb and was preparing to celebrate mightily. The telegram came as no surprise to him; he was already packed and ready to travel out with his daughter.

Then the El-Rassul, who still live in Qurna to this day, explained to me that all the tombs beneath the valley are interconnected (although all the connections have yet to be discovered) and I was able to see exactly how Carter had been able to operate all those years, invisible to everyone on the surface. For grave robbers it was perfect. They could work beneath the earth for years searching for connecting passages and blocked off doors, without the authorities having any idea that they were there.

That led me to think it through in more detail. Suppose the El-Rassul had led Carter to the entrance of Tutankhamun's tomb from one of the other tombs, say that of Ramesses VI which lies above that of Tutankhamun. Suppose they showed Carter and Carnarvon the way into the tomb, who then spent the next ten years emptying it. That would explain the 'three aeroplanes' which the locals described flying into the valley, loading up with valuables and flying out, a sighting which Carter scoffed at because it was merely the word of 'natives'.

So why, I asked myself, did Carter and Carnarvon bother to stage the discovery at all? Why not simply take all the treasure out secretly and keep it for themselves? Because, unless the tomb was officially found, they would be unable to account for any of the items and sell them openly. And because wealth wasn't their only goal. They had two objectives; the other was to obtain honour and glory. The riches they already had access to, but they could only get the glory in the eyes of the world if they announced that they had discovered the tomb of Tutankhamun, leaving enough treasure to demonstrate that it was the greatest find in the valley so far. In fact the find was so enormous that even one fifth of what was originally there was enough to make the required impact on the watching world.

But if they were to show the world the real entrance, through the empty halls already plundered by themselves and the El-Rassul, their crime would almost certainly be discovered, and even if they managed to convince the world that the robbery had happened in antiquity, the impact of the discovery would still be greatly diminished. So they would have to disguise the entrance and block off the empty rooms with false walls, moving everything into the four rooms which they were going to reveal to the world.

The opening of the Burial Chamber, like the opening of the Antechamber before it, was another magnificent piece of showmanship and illusion. Carter made the world believe that when he broke down the wall he would be in as much suspense as everyone else, that they would all be stepping back in time together, into an airless, mysterious place which had been closed up since the day of the king's burial three thousand years before.

By the time the wall was due to come down in 1923, the speculation had been whipped up to fever pitch by the press. Carter could pretend to be irked by all the ballyhoo, but in fact he had encouraged it in order to provide a smokescreen to prevent anyone looking too closely at what he was claiming he had discovered. Carter was working like a magician, using sleight of hand to distract the audience from the trick. As long as their eyes were riveted on the wall of gold appearing before them, they were paying no attention to the phoney partition wall which was fast disappearing beneath Carter's pickaxe, taking with it the evidence of who had built it. No wonder Carter and Carnarvon were feeling nervous.

When it came to dismantling the four shrines which nested within one another, in order to get to the coffin inside, Carter reported that the wood planking, though perfectly sound, had shrunk in the course of three thousand years in the dry atmosphere.[8] But the shrinking of the planking was more likely to have been caused when they were first dismantled by Carter and the El-Rassul gang. It must have proved impossible to put them back in the way they had been found, once they started taking them to pieces, especially as they had to be repositioned to conceal the original point of entry.

In his book *The Tomb of Tut-Ankh-Amen*, Carter goes on to say that the constructors of the shrine were 'past-masters in their work' and the carpentry and joinery of their constructions exhibited great skill, but that there was evidence that the obsequies had been hurried, sections having been 'banged together', regardless of the risk of damage to their gilt ornamentation. He reported deep dents from blows from a heavy hammer-like implement on the goldwork, and parts of the surfaces actually knocked off. There was, he said, workmen's refuse including chips of wood inside the shrines, which had not been cleared away.[9]

If the constructors were, as he claimed, past masters, how come the shrines were facing the wrong way, contrary to the instructions written on them? Given that these people were putting to rest their god-emperor, their beloved pharaoh, is it likely that the workmen would have been allowed to be so sloppy as to have 'banged together' sections of this most sacred shrine? Once again Carter is not only stretching the credulity of the readers, he is also insulting the holy society of Ancient Egypt with such accusations. Is it not more likely that the sloppy workmanship was that of the El-Rassul as they hurried to obey Carter's instructions during the twentieth-century plundering of the tomb?

In an interview with *The Times*, Carnarvon lamented that 'a certain amount of damp must, from some as yet unidentified source, have entered the tomb at some time, for all the linen is in practically a rotten condition'.[10]

It seems reasonable to suppose that the damp arrived in the tomb at the time Carter first entered it, bringing with him new air for the first time in three millennia. There are many corridors leading to and from the tomb, all now sealed, but once they had been opened, damp air would have entered. Up until that moment the tomb had been hermetically sealed and all within it preserved. But the lust for gold changed all that.

Carter spoke of the selectivity of the 'dynastic tomb plunderers', saying there would have been a wonderful display of riches in the treasure chests, but I am certain it was the selective activities of his own post-dynastic plunderers that had removed these great riches from those treasure caskets. He later said that at least 60 per cent of the jewellery had been taken.[11] What a sight those unplundered caskets must have presented to Carter and the El-Rassul – millions and millions in jewellery and art – the finest products of a glorious civilization all lying ready to be falsely labelled, packaged, air freighted out and sold off clandestinely to private collectors and museums.

Many of the caskets have remained in situ since their initial discovery and have only just been moved from Tomb 98 to a more secure location by the inspectors in Luxor. Despite their great provenance they stir little interest in the museums of the world. It was the treasures they once held that appeal to archaeologists. An embarrassment to the authorities, the empty caskets are a painful reminder of what was stolen.

*

Even before the official opening, Carnarvon was promising the Metropolitan Museum that he was going to let them have the lion's share of whatever was found. 'Of course,' he told Lythgoe, the museum's director, 'I will have to give something to the British Museum, but I intend to see that the Metropolitan is well taken care of.'[12]

In fact, he had no intention of selling, much less giving, any of his allocated treasure to the British Museum. The Americans paid better prices and didn't ask as many questions. At that stage Carnarvon didn't want Carter or even his own daughter, Lady Evelyn, to find out about the promise he had made to Lythgoe. Perhaps he felt they would have more scruples than he about where the artefacts went. In the end his wishes were carried out after his death and his collection was sold to the Metropolitan by his widow, Almina. Carter made the arrangements and pocketed a healthy commission for his efforts. But in the euphoria of the discovery, Carnarvon made the mistake of telling newsmen that, since the tomb had been rifled in antiquity, half the treasure was his by the terms of his contract with the Egyptian government. He also indicated that he would donate part of his share to the British Museum and the Metropolitan Museum of Art. It seems he was telling one story to one side and another to the other.

As Brackman commented in his book, *The Gold of Tutankhamun*, these remarks enraged Egyptians. *El Ahram*, an influential Egyptian journal, expressed 'doubt whether the government will take the same view' as Carnarvon. The Ministry of Public Works, of which the Department of Antiquities was a branch, put out an official statement that claimed the treasure on behalf of the Egyptian government. 'There is no question about this ... Egyptian public opinion should not be disturbed,' they stated categorically. Although regulations provided that the discoverer should receive half of the objects found in a previously plundered tomb, except for articles that the Egyptian government reserved for itself, the ministry claimed that Carnarvon's licence expressly provided that he should have no right to any objects that he might find.[13]

In a subtle ploy the government appealed to Carnarvon's sense of fair play. He, the statement alleged, had 'accepted with pleasure a condition in the licence that he was entitled to nothing (thereby) giving a clear proof that he did not entertain any material ambitions in the matter and he was devoted to the service of science and art.' This was news to both Carnarvon and Carter. Both of them wanted to appear in the eyes of the world to be totally devoted to the service of science and art. Money-grabbing, after all, was not considered to be becoming of an English gentleman. In truth, of course, the lifestyle of an English gentleman depended on the possession of considerable material wealth. And although in polite circles it was rude to speak of money or ask questions about where it came from, this was a tradition which protected those who came by it less than honestly.

So, at the time of the opening of the Burial Chamber, Carter publicly stated that he thought all the contents of the tomb 'should be placed in the Egyptian Museum' in the name of archaeology.[14] At the same time he wrote privately to Carnarvon that all efforts had to be made at the highest possible level to ensure that his lordship received a share commensurate with all the time and money he had spent. The public were also led to understand that Carter disagreed with Carnarvon about his handling of the press and the exclusive deal with *The Times*. It was whispered that this disagreement had culminated in them dissolving their partnership. In reality they were still on the best of terms at the time the press deal was done, with

Carter trying to get the most lucrative deals he could for Carnarvon for print, radio and film rights. Carter was for holding an auction and letting all the rights go to the highest bidder. At first Carnarvon agreed, then changed his mind, privately telling Carter it might appear to be too commercial.

Whatever their true positions, the deception worked and in countless articles and books such respected Egyptologists as Breasted and Gardiner portrayed Carnarvon as the one insisting on his 'pound of flesh', while Carter is depicted as jogging his lordship's elbow and insisting that all the finest pieces go to the Egyptian Museum of Antiquities.[15]

The removal of the thousands of objects officially found in the chambers (as opposed to the even greater amount already clandestinely removed), was a massive undertaking. Carter conducted it in the best military manner. Some large and heavy items had to be dismantled; the great long animal couches and the six golden chariots all had to be brought up through the narrow passageway and steep steps.[16] The scene was described by one onlooker:

> The nature of the task could hardly be imagined, everything loaded on nine cars in the early hours yesterday morning outside the tomb, everything waiting the order to proceed. To look at them one never would have thought that these matter-of-fact packages contained some of the most valuable and certainly some of the most discussed and published articles in the world today.[17]

Carter couldn't bring these large objects out the way they had really been taken in; he was pretending that the steps, sloping corridor and narrow doorway were the only entrance. Equally, he couldn't leave them in the tomb because there wasn't room and because the longer they stayed there, the more likely someone would work out that it was unlikely they had come in through the passageway, and start asking where the real entrance might be.

The tomb was closed for the season on 26 February 1923, and the corridor and entrance refilled with rubble to keep out intruders, although Carter and his team could presumably still gain access secretly through other tombs. After the hostility of the press and the political pressures of the nationalists, it must have been a relief for Carter and Carnarvon to bring the curtain down on their creation, if only for a few months. No doubt they were congratulating themselves on the stunning success of their hoax. Whatever the outcome of future disputes with the press and with Pierre Lacau and his Antiquities Service, they had pulled off the most spectacular coup imaginable and had assured themselves a place in the history books of the period.

Some of the lies which Carter and Carnarvon told have already been exposed in books like Thomas Hoving's *Tutankhamun: The Untold Story*. What Hoving and others believe happened was that the party actually spent the whole of the first night after first glimpsing the treasures inside the tomb rigging up lights and examining everything, right through to the shrine. If you believe that this actually was the day of discovery, then this theory makes sense. It is hard to imagine that after so many years of fruitless searching, they would have been able to tear themselves away from their discoveries so easily. If, as Carter and Carnarvon hold, that was truly their first glimpse into the fabulous tomb, it is unthinkable that they would just have bricked it up and gone home to bed, however tired

Carnarvon might have been after his trip from England. No one has that much self-control. These were people who looked upon the tomb as their private property and would have seen the requirement for an inspector to be there as nothing more than an annoying technicality.

But Hoving and the others were being too charitable in their judgements of our two heroes. They had, in fact, created a far more tangled web of deceit than any of their early chroniclers could imagine.

9

THE COVER-UP

Oh! What a tangled web we weave,
when first we practice to deceive.[1]
Sir Walter Scott

We need now to look a little more deeply at what was happening around Carter and Carnarvon, and work out what might have put pressure on them to cover their tracks and make their 'discovery' when they did.

In *Tutankhamun: The Untold Story*, Thomas Hoving states that in 1917 the amiable Sir Gaston Maspero retired as Director General of the Antiquities Service. To replace him he chose Pierre Lacau who, Maspero believed, would continue to look generously on the foreign archaeologists like Carter and Carnarvon, who wanted to dig in the valley. Under Maspero the arrangement had always been that anything found by excavators would be divided equally between them and the authorities unless it came from a tomb that was intact, in which case the Egyptian government would take all. Maspero had introduced the division rule in 1884 to promote scholarly work in Egypt, and decreed that foreign archaeologists should not be discouraged from digging by petty rules and regulations. It was all very vague and gentlemanly and benefited people like Carter and

Carnarvon at the expense of the Egyptians whose museums had to buy back their own national artefacts from the finders if they were going to stop them going to New York or London.

Once Lacau was in office, he showed himself in very different colours. He was a highly intelligent archaeologist and a French Jesuit obsessed with precision; it was said that he kept lists of lists. He disapproved strongly of the way in which wealthy foreigners could dig in Egypt and remove more or less what they wanted, with the authorities turning a blind eye. He believed that times had changed, that excavators should be placed under the strictest controls and never allowed to dig without an inspector present, regardless of whether they were British peers of the realm or American millionaires. He announced that from now on the Antiquities Service would appropriate all the pieces they wanted first, with the residue divided up with the finders. He also announced that he was going to tighten up the terminology about intact finds.[2] This was appalling news for Carter and Carnarvon and they took an enormous dislike to Lacau. Carter decided that he was an adversary of small intelligence, an estimation which was to prove a grave error of judgement.

In 1914, when they probably first discovered the tomb, Maspero was still in the job and the only thing Carter and Carnarvon had to worry about was ensuring that the tomb did not appear to be intact, so that they could claim at least half of whatever they showed the world they had found. Since they planned to remove most of the contents before they announced the discovery anyway, that would still mean they would end up with the vast majority of the wealth. But Lacau now looked as if he was going to be coming between them and their prize. The Metropolitan Museum was equally horrified by the proposed changes, seeing their steady supply of artefacts drying up before their eyes, and its directors tried in vain to preserve the *status quo* so that the museum could continue to receive the lion's share of the spoils from any finds in the valley, and from personal finds which dealers like Carter were able to bring to them.

Carter and Carnarvon also wanted the glory of finding an intact tomb, since none had been discovered within recorded history. They therefore had to devise a way by which they could both 'discover' an intact tomb but, at the same time, not have to hand over the remaining artefacts, *in toto*, to Lacau.

So what, I believe, they decided to do was make it look as if the tomb had been raided in antiquity. That way they could claim that it was not intact, but that it had lain as it was for three thousand years after the robbers had departed. It was not going to be hard to convince anyone that robbers had been there, since they had robbed it themselves. All they had to do was make sure that their handiwork looked three thousand years old.

In *The Tomb of Tut-Ankh-Amen*, Carter claimed that no tomb of the Eighteenth Dynasty had been robbed during the dynasty's existence because of the power and wealth of the pharaohs and their dedication to the protection of their predecessors' tombs. His argument was that there was no mention of any tomb robbery in any of the Eighteenth Dynasty documents, but plenty in the Nineteenth, Twentieth and Twenty-First. He also claimed to have found a seal impression which dated exactly the reign of Ramesses IV.[3] The reason for these, apparently trivial, arguments was that had the authorities accepted the tomb had been robbed during the Eighteenth Dynasty it would have been deemed to be technically intact and the contents entirely the property of the Egyptian government. If they agreed that it had been robbed during one of the following dynasties then equal division with the finders would operate.

Other experts, however, were not willing to simply fall into line with Carnarvon and Carter. Professor James Breasted, whose speciality was deciphering hieroglyphs and the ancient Egyptian language, later examined all the seals on the walls and doorways and declared that all were either Tutankhamun's or royal necropolis seals. He did not notice the hole made by Carter and Carnarvon, as they had concealed this and Breasted was too much of a professional to disturb items he assumed were in their original positions. He ultimately concluded that the tomb had been entered, certainly once in the Eighteenth Dynasty and maybe twice. This, according to Carter, should have been impossible. Breasted told him that the seal which Carter thought was Ramesses IV was actually a fragmented one belonging to Tutankhamun. He also disagreed with Carter's statement that no Eighteenth Dynasty tomb had ever been defiled and mentioned the one belonging to Tuthmosis IV, which had been plundered by thieves and resealed by Horemheb.[4]

'My God,' Carter is reported to have replied. 'I never thought of that.'[5] This however seems extremely unlikely, since it was Carter himself who discovered the tomb of Tuthmosis IV.

Breasted went on to advise Carter that he thought the thieves who had entered the tomb of Tuthmosis IV were not the same ones who had been caught during the start of Horemheb's reign, and pointed out that Ramesses IX's tomb lay across the entrance to the young king's, which meant that Tutankhamun's tomb had been covered over and forgotten long before Ramesses IX ruled, the time that Carter was claiming the robbery had taken place.[6]

Once again all Carter could think to reply was; 'My God, I never thought of that!'[7]

In his own book Carter does not mention Breasted's corrections but does say that he is sure the resealing of the tomb could not have taken place any later than ten years after the burial of the young king.[8] Carter, however, must have known that if Horemheb had tried to set the tomb in order after robbers had entered, it would have been earlier than ten years after the burial since the general, as soon as he assumed the throne as pharaoh, set about obliterating and erasing all mention of the rule of Tutankhamun.

It has to be borne in mind that although they did not anticipate quite so much public attention after the announcement of their discovery, Carter and Carnarvon must have known that anything they did would come under detailed scrutiny from a wide range of experts, many of whom would have vested interests in proving that the find was bogus in some way. Learned professors and museum curators are as prone to jealousy as any other group of professionals. The discoverers were going to have to make the deception very convincing if they were not to be exposed as soon as their fellow professors arrived on the scene. They had to seal up the entrance by which they had come into the tomb and disguise the true extent of the rooms, many of which now stood empty and denuded of their treasures. So they created the new entrance from a doorway which had probably originally been built as an exit, carving the steps out of the rock, and secreted the detritus which their work created beneath the floor of the Antechamber which, as a result, is a good four feet higher than the floor of the Annexe and Burial Chamber. Once the task was completed they filled the steps back in again, so that they could invent the story about their discovery by a simple water boy at a later date. They then collected all the artefacts that they had not stolen into the three rooms around the Burial Chamber – the Antechamber, the Annexe and the Treasury – piling them in the sort of haphazard manner that they hoped would suggest the tomb had been robbed in ancient times.

They also claimed that the tomb had been resealed by the priests of the time after the robbers had been and gone (remember all the seals on the opening and the block in the doorway). Is it likely, however, that priests working to restore order in the sacred tomb of a boy they saw as a sun god would have left everything piled up as if it was in someone's attic?

Then there was the matter of the chariots. Carter must have realized that someone would point out the axles were too wide to get through the doorway which he was planning to claim was the entrance. As a serious archaeologist, which he certainly was, it must have broken his heart to do it, but I believe he and his men sawed the axles in half and left them stacked against a wall. That, he must have thought, would deflect any awkward questions on that front. But it is inconceivable that the priests would have left the chariots in such a state of disarray. They would either have widened the door or, if for some reason that was impossible, they would have put the chariots back together again once they were inside the chamber, like ships in bottles. No priest would have sent the king into eternity with useless chariots.

Another problem occurred to Carter: if, as he was claiming, thieves had broken into the tomb thousands of years before, why had they not broken into the shrine with its gold coffins? It was a treasure beyond belief, so why would the robbers have ignored it? He had to think up a solution or his whole story would be thrown into question. Then it came to him. He would tell the world that the thieves didn't enter the shrine because they didn't see it. They didn't see it because it was hidden behind a wall. Carter was going to have to build a wall.

The greatest problem was to make this modern wall match the other three which surrounded the shrine and which were painted on the inside with scenes of Tutankhamun's funeral and his journey to the afterlife. The illustrated story started on the east wall, with pictures of the mummy being pulled to the tomb on a flower-bedecked shrine. The last rites were being given on the north wall and the west wall showed the pharaoh making his way to the next world. If he was going to create a south wall, Carter would have to invent a scene showing Tutankhamun arriving in the afterlife. The style of the illustrations was fairly simple and not beyond the capabilities of an artist like Carter who had been copying Egyptian art for years. To paint a wall on the inside of a sealed room, how-ever, is something of a challenge.

They built a wall to conceal the shrine but left a small hole, big enough for Carter to crawl through, allowing him to come and go during the time it took him to decorate the inside of the newly constructed wall. This task drew on all his abilities as an artist and copyist. He rose to the challenge beautifully, using all the skills he had been honing over the previous twenty-five years to create copies of designs which would convince people that the wall was solid and had always been there, and that there was only one way in and out of the Antechamber, the one he had created.

It must have been not unlike Michaelangelo's labours on the ceiling of the Sistine Chapel, but in far more cramped and over-heated conditions, crushed into the two-foot space between the outer shrine and the newly constructed wall that he was working on. For all his skills, Carter must have realized that his work would not stand up to close scrutiny. Should anyone trouble to analyse the paint, for instance, it would immediately be obvious that it was modern and not three thousand years old. He would have to ham-mer the wall down at the first opportunity under the pretext of giving access to the Burial Chamber. Had he really believed the wall was three thousand years old, is it conceivable that a craftsman as meticulous as Carter would simply have knocked it down? This was a man who we know took nearly ten years to empty and catalogue the contents of the tomb after the discovery.

But Carter left his trademark in the work: the scale he used for his painting differed from that used in the rest of the small tomb. Presumably he could not completely eradicate the style and disciplines he had been taught in England. It would probably have gone unnoticed had Harry Burton, the official dig photographer, not photographed the handiwork before it was completely demolished. Despite this, the painted figures were convincing enough to fool any layman and to escape closer scrutiny in the initial euphoria of the opening of the Burial Chamber. The official explanation for the difference in style, when it was spotted, was that the work must have been done by a different artist and in haste because the priests wanted to close the tomb up. No one in any of the books I have read ever seems to have asked the question as to how the original artists, if they had painted all four walls as claimed, were able to get out of the chamber when their work was done. Had anyone asked that question, Carter could have pointed to the hole which he himself used and they would not have had to look any further.

Nicholas Reeves notes in a book first published in 1990 called *The Complete Tutankhamun* that these figures had been 'clearly laid out by a different draughtsman, the proportions of the figures based not on the Amarna Canon of 20 squares, but upon the more traditional 18-square grid.'[9] No one else chose to pursue this mystery until three quarters of a century after Burton's damning pictures were taken. In a tomb filled with so many wonders and mysteries, who would make a fuss about one so apparently trivial?

If one accepts that the fourth wall was built and painted by Carter, the question arises of how the scenes depicted by him match so neatly with those on the other three walls, and where the original fourth wall would have been. The most likely answer is that the fourth wall was originally in the same place as Carter's partition wall, and was in fact solid rock. Carter and his team must have had a reason to remove that wall, perhaps to create the Antechamber, or connect with it so that they could move things into it. The partition wall was then erected where the original one had been.

Once Carter had arranged the tombs as he wanted them, he and his workers would have left by the new 'entrance' which they had created, Carter sealing the doors behind them as he went. The remainder of the step chippings, those not beneath the floor of the Antechamber, were mixed with other detritus and left in the tunnel. The tomb was now ready to be 'discovered', an immaculately conceived and staged piece of theatre, as artfully forged as any work of art before or since.

When later describing his feelings at the moment of opening up the first doorway, Carter said that there was always the 'horrible possibility' that the sanctuary might be unfinished or incomplete. 'The door to the tomb was really too small for the tomb of a king.'[10] If these doubts truly assailed him, why had he been so confident in his telegram to Carnarvon? 'At last have made wonderful discovery in Valley; a magnificent tomb with seals intact...'[11] He was so confident because he knew exactly what he was going to find, but he wanted to forestall other doubters who might suspect that the tomb complex was incomplete. In reality the complex appeared unfinished because most of the rooms had been sealed off by Carter's men and the entrance was too small because it was not the real entrance. By pretending to be worried about what he would find, Carter hoped to deflect possible accusations that the whole tomb was indeed a fake.

Once the day of discovery had passed (without an inspector in attendance despite Lacau's instructions) Carter set about using all his abilities to create a show that would distract everyone from asking too many questions, a skill which he had demonstrated many times before. When Carter was working for Theodore Davis, one of Davis's companions described how another tomb looked once Carter had been there:

> We entered Amenhotep's tomb – now lighted with electricity, showing arrangements and decoration delightfully. The rifled mummy had been restored to his sarcophagus, and decently wrapped with the torn mummy cloth – and Carter has arranged the whole thing most artistically. A shrouded electric light is at the head of the sarcophagus throwing the fine face into splendid relief – and when all the other lights were extinguished, the effect was solemn and impressive. Carter has done wonderful work over there [in the Valley] in a dozen different ways ... No more stumbling about amongst yawning pits and rough stair cases, with flickering candles dripping wax all over one.[12]

When it came to working the same magic on Tutankhamun, he was ably assisted by the contents of the tomb themselves which, particularly when skilfully lit, were so breathtakingly beautiful they distracted anyone from asking awkward questions. Everyone was so dazzled they never thought to doubt the truth of what they were seeing.

One of the reasons it took Carter ten years to clear out the contents of the tomb was the meticulous way in which he insisted every object should be listed, sketched and photographed at every stage. Looking now at the pictures which Harry Burton took when Carter first started to sort through the random piles of goods and chattels, with each item numbered, one is unavoidably reminded of police 'scene of crime' pictures which, I believe, is effectively what they are. Carter however, claimed it was the scene of a crime committed three thousand years ago. He even described how he believed the robbers had worked in the Annexe.

> One robber – there would probably not have been room for more than one – had crept into the chamber, and had then hastily but systematically ransacked its entire contents, empty-ing boxes, throwing things aside, piling them one upon another, and occasionally passing objects through the hole to his companions for closer examinations in the outer chamber. He had done his work just about as thoroughly as an earth-quake.[15]

Carter deliberately let slip to fellow workers and confidants like Carnarvon's half-brother, that he had been into the Burial Chamber before the official opening. By doing that he was able to explain the hole in the wall and why it had been covered by the basket and rushes, saying that he had made the hole in order to get in from the Antechamber, having abandoned his first story, that it had been made by tomb robbers. In fact, the hole had been created for Carter to get out of the Burial Chamber after painting the inside of the wall.

By admitting he had been unable to resist the temptation to take a peek, he made the story of the discovery all the more believable.

How many of us would have been able to resist such a temptation? How many of us would approve of the bravado of the adventurers who refused to wait for the bureaucratic and small-minded inspectors to arrive? By confessing to this minor, infinitely understandable technical misdemeanour, he made himself appear all the more honest and all the more endearingly human.

But, when analysed in even the most casual manner, the story of the four of them – Carter, Carnarvon, Lady Evelyn and Pecky Callender – peering through a hole in the wall on the night of the discovery, with nothing more than a candle and a torch to illuminate the wonders before them, shows itself to be a nonsense. They claimed they could see the two life-sized sentinels standing either side of the blocked entrance to the Burial Chamber, but there is no way they could have seen them from where they were. Later scholars might put this fabrication down to Carter's wish to hide the fact that they actually went into the tomb that evening without an inspector in tow. I believe it is just one more piece of evidence that demonstrates the entire business of the discovery was a sham, devised as a smokescreen to distract attention from what had really happened.

Hearing there were rumours circulating about how they had been plundering the tomb, secretly filling aeroplanes with treasure, and knowing that Pierre Lacau was now on the warpath, Carter and Carnarvon decided to stage another show to distract attention. They announced the official opening of the tomb. They may have intended it as a gesture of openness but to the rest of the world it seemed elitist and exclusive. As previously noted, the only newspaperman they invited was Arthur Merton from *The Times*, in accordance with the deal that Carnarvon had struck with his employers. On top of that, neither Lacau nor his assistant, Paul Tottenham, were invited to the ceremony. Carter and Carnarvon did not even inform the Antiquities Service of the opening. Perhaps they considered it their tomb and they could invite whoever they chose, or maybe they didn't want Lacau to see too much until they had had a chance to muddy the waters still further. Either way, it was a serious error and one they would pay dearly for in the not too distant future.

The evening before the opening, Carter sent a note to the designated inspector, Rex Englebach, explaining that all was now clear for him to make a final inspection. The note was delivered too late in the evening for Englebach to respond and, because he was busy on other sites, he was also not able to come to the tomb for the opening. Instead, he sent a local inspector, Ibrahim Effendi, in his place.

At the opening ceremony, Carter continued the theatre. After a brief greeting to the assembled group, he said, 'Are we ready? Come please.'[14] He then led them down the stairs and along the passageway to a huge steel gate which he had erected at the inner doorway and draped for the occasion in a white sheet. The lights inside the tomb had been turned on and emitted a muted glow from within. Carter stopped. Then, after advising his audience where the robbers' hole had been made, he whisked aside the sheet. A great gasp of wonder went up from the crowd and many of them later reported just what a staggering sight they beheld. All had been illuminated and the gleaming gold and multicoloured objects in the tomb had been artistically lit to show them to their best advantage. Carter increased the drama further by delaying the opening of the steel door for as long as possible, dragging great chains around the bars. The show was well and truly on the road.

After the opening, Carter was inundated with offers of help, many of which he gratefully accepted. Letters poured in from all over the world, from cranks and souvenir hunters, as well as people wanting to join the group. There were letters from church groups condemning the opening of a sacred tomb and any number of people claiming kinship to Carter. Against this background he was working frantically with his growing staff. A huge amount of equipment had to be ordered in: all manner of stores, electrical power and photographic equipment.

His greatest benefactor, the Metropolitan Museum, wasted no time in putting their people in place, and urged the US State Department to put maximum pressure on the Egyptian government to ensure that nothing untoward was done to stop the equal division of tomb contents between the finders and the government. They knew that if Carter and Carnarvon were able to get their hands on half the goods, the Metropolitan stood a good chance of being able to buy them. If everything went to the museum in Cairo they would be cut out.

Carter had very definite ideas as to how he would clear the tomb. He was a methodical perfectionist and this was his finest hour. Nothing was going to be allowed to spoil it. Nothing and nobody. He received permission to use three other tombs in the vicinity as storerooms, laboratories and a darkroom. They were the tomb of Seti II, an unfinished and unmarked tomb simply designated tomb 15, and the tomb that Davis had found many years before and believed was the tomb of Akhenaten, tomb 55.[15] These tombs were of vital importance to Carter, part of his master plan to continue the greatest deception in the history of Egyptology.

In the tomb of Seti II there are some paintings which appear identical with many of the portraits and statues of Tutankhamun found in his tomb. This seems like too much of a coincidence. I am certain that the Seti II tomb, like many others, links to the tomb of

Tutankhamun as part of the greater complex. By using it as a laboratory and ensuring that it was barred, bolted and padlocked at all times, Carter was able to stop anyone else from examining it. This also meant that he probably had secret access through to Tutankhamun's tomb should he need it. Winlock states that the Bank of England was not better protected than Carter's laboratory, nor more time-consuming to enter.

Once the removal of the tomb contents was under way, Carnarvon returned to Egypt after an absence of over a month and headed towards the valley, accompanied by Lady Evelyn in an automobile which Carter had purchased. Over glasses of champagne the team was toasted and in an interview with Arthur Merton the earl observed:

> What I have to say may, perhaps, be interesting, because the objects are now much more easily examined and appreciated, and no authoritative description of any individual objects has yet been published.
>
> I went first to the tomb of Seti II, which is now used, as is known, as a workshop or laboratory. Here I was able to see and study the results of the labours of Mr Carter and his assistants. We have to be very careful as to who approaches even the entrance of the laboratory, but admission is not in itself a pleasure. Even from the outside the smell of chemicals is perceptible, and on entering, the odours of acetone, collodion and other unpleasant things which the experts seem to enjoy using are very strong. The tomb consists of what, in effect, is a long passageway, and all the way down are boxes containing precious objects. There are tables covered with bottles, large parcels of wadding and trays containing miscellaneous objects

lightly covered with cloths to keep off the dust. The door through which you enter has a very ponderous steel gate with four padlocks, which we hope precludes any possibility of theft. Altogether, nothing could be more admirably arranged than the details over which Mr Carter and his staff have spent so much thought and labour. The passage is a long one, running into the hillside, and the only light comes from the entrance. At the farther end one must examine the objects with an electric torch.

You have already heard of the throne or chair of state. It is even more beautiful than we had imagined; the delicacy of the inlaid precious stone work is quite extraordinary, and the carving and modelling of the figures of the King and Queen, which are in low relief, are really wonderful in power and expression. I believe it is the only example of such a chair of state yet found. Between the seat and the legs were originally figures or decorative work of some kind, probably of gold, because they have been torn away by robbers. From the struts supporting and strengthening the legs jagged ends show where the figures have been roughly broken off. Great care must necessarily be exercised in handling the restoration of this beautiful object, because some parts of it are in a most delicate condition.[16]

The original figures most certainly were made of gold, which is probably why they were taken, but Carnarvon is displaying the most terrible hypocrisy here. He says the throne was very beautiful, the inlaid work quite extraordinary, the only chair of state ever found. Yet it is callously broken and the gold figures snapped off, almost certainly by Carter and his team. Those figures were worth a fortune. Lythgoe subsequently secured the squatting statue of Tutankhamun from the open market for the Metropolitan Museum. How did it get onto the open market? Who sold it? And by what right? It can only have been Carnarvon or Carter.

At the time many people complained about the obsessive secrecy of the laboratory assistants working with Mace and Lucas. Mace was Carter's right-hand man and knew what was going on. Lucas was a brilliant chemist from Manchester who was kept at a distance from the proceedings. But, as we have seen, this secrecy was crucial if Carter was to ensure that those with the knowledge to expose him were not allowed to get too close to the truth.

In his book on the discovery, *The Tomb of Tut-Ankh-Amen*, Carter likened clearing the objects from the Antechamber to playing a gigantic game of Spillikins, a game sometimes called 'pick-a-stick' where you scatter a pile of sticks on top of one another and have to pick up as many as possible without moving others. 'So crowded were they [the treasures] that it was hard to move one without serious risk of damaging others. In some cases they were so inextricably tangled that an elaborate system of props and supports had to be devised to hold one object or group of objects in place while another was being removed.'[17]

In general, Carter used his series of books to promote his hypotheses as if they were unassailable facts. He talked about the thieves in ancient times penetrating the tomb through a small tunnel as if that was definitely what had happened, which I believe it certainly was not. If the supposed thieves had penetrated into all the chambers of the tomb as Carter at one point claimed – thereby destroying his earlier defence that the Burial Chamber had remained untouched because it was hidden behind the wall – they would surely have ransacked the golden shrines. In *The Tomb of*

Tut-Ankh-Amen, Carter claimed that the shrines had been left intact by the ancient thieves, although many things had been taken from the small storeroom but admitted a little damage had been done to the shrine's folding doors by 'predatory intruders' for the purpose of 'peering in'.[18] The fact that the shrines were not violated, even after supposedly being discovered by ancient thieves, is proof positive that the only thieves who had entered the tomb were Carter and his team.

In another sentence, Carter suggests that had it not been for the discovery of the tunnel and resealed doorway, he might have assumed that the confusion of the Antechamber was due to 'Oriental carelessness at the time of the funeral'.[19] Is it feasible for one second that the priestly followers of the pharaoh, entombing for eternity their beloved god-king, would leave a scene of confusion to accompany him throughout eternity? This was a solemn holy ceremony carried out with all the reverence that ancient Egypt could accord to their dead monarch. Everything was positioned in its proper place and the priests ensured that this was done with meticulous attention to detail.

Carter talked about the things which he believed the thieves had taken. He explained that within the small gold shrine there was a pedestal of gilded wood for a statuette, with the imprint of the statuette's feet still marked on it. The statuette itself was gone and Carter believed there could be very little doubt that it was a solid gold one, 'probably very similar to the gold statuette of Thothmes III, in the image of Amun, in the Carnarvon collection'. The little gold statue which was the pride of Carnarvon's collection and is now in the Metropolitan Museum in New York almost certainly came from the shrine in Tutankhamun's tomb before the official discovery. Carter also said that, 'Many objects of solid gold were overlooked.' This was most certainly not the case. Virtually all of the gold objects were removed and sold and anything that was left was for the purposes of creating a smokescreen.

Carter often anticipated the questions that arose in the minds of other experts by stating them boldly in his books as his own concerns. He tells his readers that the tomb is not at all like the normal Theban tombs but quite a simple affair. He points out that it is orientated in the standard way, painted the normal colour and has the four magical figures placed at the cardinal points.[20] But although the orientation of the tomb is correct, the golden shrines were wrongly placed. They should have faced towards the Kingdom of the Dead – the west – but this would have led people to wonder what was beyond the west wall. With the shrine pointing east it faced the Treasury and answered the questions before they were asked.

Carter also stated that the Antechamber and Burial Chamber were continuous except for the partition wall (which he had built) and a drop of four feet in the floor level from the former to the latter, but he never attempted to explain why that might be. I believe the reason that the floor of the Antechamber is not on the same level as the Burial Chamber and the other chambers is that it was not originally part of the tomb. Like the partition wall, it may have been a construction by Carter. When he talks about the partition wall in his book, Carter says that it must have been built after the interment of the king, suggesting the sealing was done by the departing priests when of course it was actually done by Carter himself. He acknowledges that the plastering and painting of the shrine was executed under difficult conditions. One wall certainly was, the dividing wall between the Antechamber and the Burial Chamber. He admitted that the figures on the wall had a 'crudeness of workmanship'. It must have galled Carter to have to decry his own craft, but he had to say it before anyone else did and started to question why the work was so crude.

When describing the chaos in the Annexe, Carter wrote, 'The scene, in fact, seemed almost as if contrived, with theatrical artifice, to produce a state of bewilderment upon the beholder.'[21] The scene was contrived and with great theatrical artifice, by Carter himself. It was supposed to bewilder the beholder and it succeeded eminently, along with all his other contrivances. However, I believe that during the period that they were setting up their elaborate hoax, Carter and Carnarvon uncovered something which neither of them knew how to deal with.

During the ten years that they were emptying and studying the tomb, I believe that they discovered a secret which was to add yet another layer to the web of lies and subterfuge that was growing around those four small rooms, a web that within months of the opening would lead to the murder of Carnarvon and others, crimes attributed to the 'mummy's curse'.

I have talked at length to many people considered experts on the subject of Tutankhamun and the period surrounding his discovery. All of them have confirmed to me the facts as they know them and have agreed that my theories explain a lot that has puzzled other thinkers on the subject over the years.

In 1996 I visited the Valley of the Kings with some friends with the intention of examining as many tombs as possible. The tomb of Ramesses VI which had been closed for fifteen years had just been reopened. This was the tomb which lay across the top of Tutankhamun's and the one through which I believed Carter and Carnarvon had found their way. I suggested to my companions that we should look for a gap or plastered-over portion at the entrance, which would be where they found their way into Tutankhamun's tomb. Sure enough, 150 feet into the entrance, on the right, in a cordoned-off area, was a portion of unpainted and unadorned wall. On the left-hand side of this otherwise blank area was some hieroglyphic writing which looked as if it had been left unfinished. I felt entirely sure that this was the original entrance to the tomb of Tutankhamun.

Later, in Tutankhamun's Antechamber, I tapped with my knuckle on the south wall. It gave off a cracked sound which confirmed that it was not solid. It looked as if it had been plastered over and painted a dull yellow in keeping with the rest of the Antechamber. The distance from that point to the blocked entrance in Ramesses's tomb is about thirty feet. That, I believe, is the corridor through which the worldly goods of the dead king were brought.

In a westerly direction, about a hundred yards away, lies the tomb of Horemheb which I believe may also have been part of the Tutankhamun complex. A direct line drawn between the accepted tombs of Tutankhamun and Horemheb bisects the cache which Davis discovered and believed to be the actual tomb of the young pharaoh, and probably was an integral part of it.

Perhaps it is now impossible to completely disentangle all the possibilities and probabilities after millennia of confusion and deception, but it is quite certain that the story which Carter and Carnarvon were telling the world, of the first discovery of the tomb, was not the truth.

10

HOWARD CARTER'S
GRAND FINALE

The sarcophagus lid trembled, began to rise.
Slowly, and swaying uncertainly, it swung clear.
At first we saw only a long, narrow, black void. Then across
the middle of this blackness we gradually discerned fragments
of granite which had fallen out of the fracture in the lid. They
were lying scattered upon a dark shroud through which
we seemed to see emerging an indistinct form . . .[1]

James Breasted

The digging season following Carnarvon's death began smoothly enough. A renewal of Carnarvon's concession was applied for by his widow, and Carter was appointed to advise and continue with the work of clearance – all of which was acceptable to the Antiquities Service. The agreement with *The Times* was renewed, for a second year, and this time Arthur Merton was taken on as an official member of the excavating team. Carter believed that he had to do this in order to limit the constant stream of visitors, official and otherwise, and despite the uproar which it had caused the previous year. He thought that Merton could deflect the press's attention from himself.

With the unveiling of the pharaoh's mummy, the show was back on the road with a vengeance, and the world's attention focused on the valley once more as Carter descended into the Burial Chamber and prepared to disclose what was hidden within the first golden shrine. Just as with the openings of the Antechamber and the Burial Chamber, the opening of the shrines, sarcophagus and coffins was a momentous event. The locks on the first shrine were already undone. Carter claimed it was the work of the ancient grave robbers, but, as I have suggested, it was more likely the work of his own men. The second shrine appeared to have remained bolted since the interment of the king.

With the tension mounting, Carter and his team slid back the bolts on the doors of the second shrine, cutting both ends of the securing entwined ropes and swinging open the doors, allowing the bright electric lights to flood on to the fabulously carved gold-leafed façade of the third shrine which lay within, supposedly exposed for the first time in three thousand years. When they opened the third door they found a fourth shrine, covered in writing. Professor Newberry stepped forward to translate the most prominent hieroglyphs for the select company. He worked in silence for a few minutes and then whispered the words to the group: 'I have seen yesterday; I know tomorrow.'[2]

It was time to open what everyone assumed would be the last shrine, the one that would finally reveal whether the king's sarcophagus and coffin were still lying where the priests had placed them. Carter wrote:

The decisive moment was at hand! An indescribable moment for the archaeologist! What was beneath and what did the shrine contain? With intense excitement I drew back the bolts of the last and unsealed doors; they slowly swung open, and there, filling the entire area within, effectually barring any further progress, stood an immense pink quartzite sarcophagus, intact, with the lid still firmly fixed in its place, just as the pious hands had left it.[5]

A carved arm stretched out from the sarcophagus towards the invaders. The tension was building all the time. The heat under the lights must have been gruelling. The audience could now be certain that there was a magnificent sarcophagus there, intact.

'When Carter and I opened the doors of the third and fourth shrines and beheld the massive sarcophagus within,' Breasted wrote, 'I felt for the first time the majesty of the dead Pharaoh's actual presence.'

The crowds outside the tomb swelled as people waited for more news of the discoveries within.

When asked what he expected to find, Carter replied, 'Something almost unimaginable. I hope to find a series of gold coffins, possibly three, and the intimate treasures of the dead king – particularly the double crown of Upper and Lower Egypt, the pharaonic regalia and the royal jewels. More fervently, I long to discover papyri which might cast additional light on the king who, among all his objects, was still not more than a shadow.'[4] But Carter already knew what was inside the shrines because he had already had them to pieces in the years before he and Carnarvon shared their discovery with the world. I believe he also knew who the king really was and his extraordinary place in world mythology, because he had seen the papyri from the kilts of the sentinels, papyri which had since disappeared.

The strain of carrying the sole responsibility for the work, and the truth, without the support of his partner and confidant must have been hard for Carter. It is also possible that he was aware his life might be in danger because of what he knew. That too might have been on his mind as he worked. He must have felt very isolated as he toiled on in the barren desert, despite the glory of his fame. Commentators who saw him in this period, walking around in the heat of the desert in his heavy English tweeds, reported that his face looked drawn.

The team dismantled the first two shrines and then once more progress was halted as they planned how to dismantle the final two shrines in order to reach the sarcophagus which they could now see within.

The world outside waited and watched.

A few days later the team resumed the work, peeling yet more layers from the onion as they moved towards the pink sarcophagus at the core.[5] The lid of the sarcophagus, which would most likely have been made either of solid gold or from quartzite like the sarcophagus itself, was no longer there and had been replaced by an ill-fitting granite one.

The switch could only have been made by Carter and his men during their decade of tomb robbery, certainly not by the pious hands which Carter had referred to. Perhaps the temptation of such a colossal piece of gold proved too much for them to resist. Or perhaps it bore writing which confirmed the frightening secrets which they had discovered in the papyri – about who the occupant really was – and had to be disposed of. Either way, it is hard to imagine how else such an inappropriate lid could have found its way on to the sarcophagus. In carrying out the switching of the lids, the robbers had even managed to break the granite replacement in two and, to this day, it lies on the floor of the tomb as mute testimony to their deed.

In his writings, Carter explained that the cracks across the lid had been carefully cemented and painted over to disguise the damage. He is clear that the lid had not been tampered with since the burial and suggests that the priests who buried the pharaoh had initially intended to have a quartzite lid to match the sarcophagus, but that some accident must have occurred which meant they had to find a substitute. Or perhaps, he proposed, the intended lid had not been ready in time for the burial and the crudely made granite slab had had to be used instead.

Once again, he managed to deflect potential doubts by stating the obvious himself before anyone else could. If, as I believe, the cementing and painting was done by Carter himself, it would be relatively simple to prove: a small sample of the cement, if analysed, would show it to be of a twentieth-century manufacture.

Carter pointed out that the shrines were just as the Egyptian masons left them, even to the last few flakes of limestone from their chisels which lay on the floor. It seems more likely to me that the El-Rassul family would have left that sort of mess when they were carrying out Carter's instructions, than the priests and craftsmen who were burying their pharaoh with pious hands.

Whatever the state of the lid, its removal constituted the next cliffhanger for everyone watching inside and waiting in the valley. What would they find inside? Would it be empty, or just a pile of rotted linen? Or would they find the body of the king still intact and surrounded by more evidence of his fabulous wealth? To find out they had to lift the mighty lid. Carter devised a complicated system of pulleys and ropes and later described the moment when the lid started to rise, tears coming to his eyes as he remembered his feelings at the time.

The lid was raised, disclosing a colossal mummy case, seven feet four inches long and fashioned from heavily gilded wood, carved in the likeness of the monarch as the god Osiris. The hands were crossed upon the chest, the right holding the emblematic flail, and the left the crooked sceptre, both of gold and faience. The face, a remarkable portrait, was formed of solid gold with eyes of crystal, and on the forehead was the sacred serpent and a vulture of gold and faience, while on each side was the figure of a goddess with arms and wings out-stretched.[6]

This latest revelation more than satisfied the crowds waiting outside the tomb in the sun and the many more who were following in their newspapers at home. More and more tourists poured into Luxor, overwhelming the supply of hotel rooms. Those who were able to dispense the biggest backhanders won out as the locals cashed in on the gold rush. The local traders in real and fake antiquities did a roaring trade, shipping in artefacts from all over the country to sell to the hordes of visitors. The find was as spectacular as everyone had hoped it would be, and as Carter had known it would be. The golden image that would become so familiar to the world had been glimpsed by the world for the first time in three millennia.[7]

With the lid hovering in mid-air, the team stopped work once more to take stock of the situation.

However well things seemed to be going for Carter in the tomb, outside they were going badly. He had made a number of unwise decisions, most importantly continuing the contract with *The Times* and fighting with Lacau over the division of the spoils. The pressures were building. There were endless meetings, demands, discussions, agreements, compromises and obstructions. For a man who just wanted to get on with his work in the tomb, the frustrations must have been intolerable. Mentally drained by the endless difficulties and trivial demands emanating from the Ministry of Public Works and the Antiquities Service, and physically exhausted by the awesome responsibility of dismantling the fragile shrines, Carter finally snapped in the middle of the opening of the sarcophagus.

The trivial straw that broke the camel's back was the refusal of the Egyptian authorities to allow the wives of the excavators a special visit to the tomb to view the sarcophagi. Carter chose to take the refusal as an insult to English women in general and the wives of his colleagues in particular. He might have been appalled by the superior attitudes of his compatriots towards local workers, but he shared their contempt for Egyptian bureaucrats who, in the parlance of the day, quite simply did not know their place.

Bolstered by bad advice, on 12 February 1924 Carter downed tools, leaving the heavy lid of Tutankhamun's sarcophagus suspended perilously above the king's shrouded form on the complicated system of pulleys and ropes. Marching furiously into Luxor he posted a notice in the crowded lobby of the Winter Palace Hotel, apparently expecting everyone else to be as incensed as he himself was by this insulting turn of events.

Owing to the impossible restrictions and discourtesies of the Egyptian Public Works Department and its antiquities service, all my collaborators, as a protest, have refused to work any further upon their scientific investigations in the tomb.[8]

He must have believed that when they were so close to the final prize, the authorities would do everything in their power to appease him and coax him back to work. If he was thinking rationally at all by that stage he must have decided that it was a gamble worth taking. But he too must have been anxious to open the coffins and reveal to the world the wonders which he knew awaited within. By withdrawing now he risked giving the final prize to someone else who might be brought in by the Antiquities Service to complete the task. These were the crowning moments of his long career, why would he risk losing them? It was the first strike in archaeological history, precipitated by a childish tantrum and then prolonged by Carter's infamous stubbornness. He was banking on the power of the British and American establishments to force the Egyptian politicians to bow to his demands. It would prove to be a big mistake.

If Carnarvon had still been alive such a confrontation almost certainly wouldn't have happened; the earl would have found a way of defusing the tension with a mixture of charm and influence. But he was not there and Carter lacked the requisite skills to avert a headlong collision. All the stubbornness of his nature was combined with the arrogance of a man who believed that the tomb belonged to him and the exhaustion of an archaeologist working conscientiously beyond his powers of endurance.

Lacau and the Egyptian authorities were delighted by this rash display of temper: Carter had played directly into their hands. If he was bluffing they were quite happy to call that bluff. The Egyptians had had enough of this sort of high-handed behaviour by foreigners in their country. Carter's precipitate action resulted in the contract for the Carnarvon concession being deemed broken and it was duly revoked by Pierre Lacau, who announced that the Egyptians would finish the work themselves.

Rather than being seen as the victim of the situation, as a selfless scholar wishing nothing more than to be allowed to get on with the job in peace, Carter, who had done nothing to win the goodwill of the world's press, became the villain of the piece. He could be depicted as mindlessly putting at risk the boy king's treasures to make his own petty point. One by one his friends and supporters began to distance themselves from him. In desperation he resorted to that bluntest of implements, the courts. Everyone was horrified. Percy Newberry even received a telegram from Downing Street asking him to, 'Urge Carter on highest authority to stop legal proceedings. Make amicable arrangement with Egyptian authorities.'[9]

But, as usual, Carter was not to be deflected and on 25 February 1924, he went with Mace to instruct solicitors. As late as 8 March, Whitehall was still trying to contact Almina Carnarvon to persuade her to intervene with Carter, but she was on her way to South Africa and could not be reached.

The court case came up and then, just as an acceptable compromise was coming into sight, Carter's English lawyer, F. M. Maxwell, made an ill-considered reference to the Egyptian government, now headed by the ultra-nationalist prime minister Said Zaghlul. The premier was a man who had once been imprisoned by the British and someone who Maxwell, in an earlier case, had sought to have hanged as a terrorist; it would be impossible to overstate the sensitivities upon which the lawyer was trampling. In defending Carter's actions, Maxwell stood up in a public court, with all the world's journalists listening, and claimed that the Egyptian government 'had come in like a pack of bandits and forced him [Carter] out of possession by violence'.[10]

The Arabic word for bandit or thief is one of the worst insults you can level at a man. The uproar was colossal. At a time of intense anti-British feeling in the country, the insult, perceived as directed at all Egyptians, provoked rioting in the streets and worsened Carter's situation a hundredfold. The British government were also now after his blood, furious that he had upset delicate diplomatic relations with his arrogance. And then, just as it looked as if things couldn't get any worse, they did.

According to Thomas Hoving in *Tutankhamun: The Untold Story*, when Carter left Egypt a special commission of Egyptians headed by Pierre Lacau was formed to make an inventory of the tomb. An official inspection of Carter's original storeroom, on 30 March 1924, brought to light a wonderful and undocumented sculpture of Tutankhamun. The head, it seemed, had been deliberately hidden in a Fortnum and Mason's crate marked 'Red Wine'. One of the finest pieces of art to come from the entire hoard, it was almost life-sized and carved from wood, then covered with a layer of plaster and painted so perfectly that it appeared almost alive.[11] The features were handsome and seemed to belong to a young boy. The head was emerging from the petals of a blue lotus blossom, a flower which, according to Egyptian folklore, was the first to appear in the pool of creation. It was a beautifully carved image of the birth of the Son of God, an illustration of the ancient text: 'He who emerged from the lotus upon the High Mount, who illumines with his eyes, the Two Lands'.[12]

Lacau and his fellow inspectors were horrified. What could this mean? Had Carter and his team been intending to steal this fabulous piece? Why was it not listed anywhere? Had the English been planning to spirit it away in a wine crate? Would it have disappeared into some private collection? If these suspicions were true the ramifications were unthinkable. What else might the team have stolen?

By this time Carter was out of the country, but all hell broke loose. The authorities clearly believed that Carter had concealed the piece intentionally. Herbert Winlock, who was in charge of the Metropolitan Museum's Egyptian expedition, did his best to dig Carter out of the mess, suggesting in a coded message to him that Carter might perhaps say that he had acquired the piece for Lord Carnarvon from unofficial excavations at the site of El-Amarna in 1923. Carter rejected this alibi, stating that the head did come from the Tutankhamun tomb and had been discovered in the debris of the tomb corridor. His explanation, though less than convincing, was willingly accepted by the Antiquities Service who had as much interest in avoiding a full-scale scandal as the Metropolitan. However, the very fact that Winlock and Carter had a private code through which they could communicate in secret says a great deal about the way in which the museums of the western world were working with the excavators to the detriment of the local authorities.

The discovery of the tomb of Tutankhamun had turned from a triumph of romance and adventure into a continuing international incident involving the English, American, French and Egyptian governments. (The French were the ruling European body in Egypt, and had been since the time of Napoleon. This had been agreed to by Great Britain when the German colonies in Africa were divided between France and England.) For the moment, Carter found himself out in the cold and his anger was at boiling point. He decided to set the record straight in a 74-page pamphlet clumsily entitled 'The Tomb of Tut. Ank. Amen, Statement, with Documents, as to the events which occurred in Egypt in the Winter of 1923–24, leading to the ultimate break with the Egyptian Government'.[15]

It was Carter's apologia for the sorry mess in which he found

himself and a justification of the firm stand he had taken with those
– principally Pierre Lacau – whose sole, spiteful aim, he claimed,
was to make a difficult task more difficult still. The statement rolled
off the presses in early June, just as significant progress was being
made on Carter's behalf by his few remaining supporters in Cairo.
Despite the limited distribution of a few dozen copies, the unex-
pected appearance of the statement caused a new furore, and not
only among Carter's enemies. Winlock, hitherto one of Carter's
staunchest allies, was horrified to find himself implicated, in an
appendix, in the mess of the crated head and coded message. He
immediately withdrew his support. Surprised by Winlock's reaction, the insensitive Carter merely offered to remove the offending
text from those copies still to be distributed. The gesture cut little
ice; the damage had already been done. Other supporters were
more philosophical. For James Breasted, another exasperated supporter of Carter if only for his own political ends, 'The Summary
will always be a monument in the history of research in the Near
East.'[14]

Despite appearances to the contrary, Winlock's rejection pulled
Carter up sharp. Without the support of the Metropolitan he would
be truly out in the wilderness. With the intervention of Edward
Robinson, Director of the Metropolitan and a calming voice of
reason, the troublesome Egyptologist was persuaded to suppress his
controversial pamphlet altogether. He also agreed to withdraw from
his ill-starred legal confrontation with Lacau and the Egyptian
government. Carter realized he had gone as far as he could and,
with time, the problems surrounding the find slowly began to resolve themselves. Carter agreed to renounce all personal claim to
the antiquities in the tomb; he wrote a letter to Pierre Lacau.[15]

I, the undersigned, Howard Carter, definitely renounce any action, claim, or pretension whatsoever, both as regards the Tomb of Tut-Ankh-Amun and the objects therefrom and also in respect of the cancellation of the authorisation of the measures taken by the government in consequence of such cancellation. I declare that I withdraw all actions pending and I authorise the representative of the government to apply for them to be struck out.[16]

Almina followed suit, although the Carnarvon estate refused to drop its claim to some form of compensation and was eventually awarded the sum of £56,000 which was estimated to cover the costs which Carnarvon had incurred in his treasure hunting. The fact that he had made millions from stolen artefacts was not taken into consideration.[17]

In November 1924 politics intervened once more. The British commander-in-chief of the Egyptian army, Sir Lee Stack, was assassinated, resulting in the installation of a new, pro-British government. Zaghlul and the nationalists were out. Carter, though in a stronger position now than he had been for many months, nevertheless decided to stand by his letter to Lacau. He had simply lost the will to fight. He agreed not to renew *The Times* monopoly for a third season and meekly accepted nominal government supervision of his work in the form of an Antiquities Service inspector, Rushdi Effendi. After the months of swagger and obstinacy, Carter had been tamed and control was now firmly in the hands of the Egyptians, who, in turn, had been unable to find anyone who wanted to take on Carter's arduous workload and must have been deeply relieved when he finally caved in so easily.[18]

Howard Carter's Grand Finale

On 25 January 1925, Carter could at last return to the tomb to concentrate on what he did best – archaeology. Taking up where he had left off the previous year, he returned to the hazardous task of un-nesting the coffins from within the sarcophagus. His first task would be to lift the lid of the first gilded coffin which he had uncovered a year earlier. On 13 October 1925 Carter staged the final act of his great performance. By his own admission, 'it was a moment as anxious as exciting', as the outermost lid of the coffin was finally lifted by its four silver handles. How many more coffins would there be inside? Once again the world watched enthralled as he set to work.

Inside was a second coffin, shrouded in linen and covered in garlands of flowers. As he gently rolled the shrouds back Carter revealed what he later described as 'the finest example of the ancient coffin-maker's art ever yet seen'.[19] This lid also depicted the king as Osiris, but it was made to an even higher standard than the first. It was six feet, eight inches long, fitting snugly into the outer coffin, made of thick gold foil, lavishly inlaid with engraved glass jewels.

It took a team of eight men all their strength to lift the coffins out of the sarcophagus so that they could work on them. The enormous weight suggested, to those who didn't already know, that there was going to be more to find inside.

When the second coffin lid was lifted another human image emerged from the distant past, swathed in gossamer linen shrouds. Carter rolled back more fragile material and lifted an elaborate bead and floral collar surrounding the neck to reveal the third coffin, made of solid gold, half an inch thick in some places and six feet long. It was, as Carter later put it, 'an absolutely incredible mass of pure bullion'.[20] The gold was exquisitely decorated with inlays. 'How great,' Carter later wrote, 'must have been the wealth buried with those ancient Pharaohs! What riches that Valley must have once concealed!'[21]

The strange thing about the faces carved on the coffins was that they didn't appear to be portraits of the same person. The second coffin, it seemed, might not have been intended for Tutankhamun at all. Perhaps it was his brother, Smenkhkara, whose mummy has never been found. Carter's explanation for this anomaly was that the priests were not expecting Tutankhamun to die so young and so had not prepared everything in readiness for his entombing. They therefore had to use another coffin. Alternatively, there may have been some rearranging done by Carter and the El-Rassul, for what reason we can only guess at. Could it be that they wanted to switch the heads around in order to confuse anyone trying to prove who the body belonged to? It seems to me likely that the tomb which Carter and Carnarvon revealed to the world was not Tutankhamun's at all, but that of his brother. I believe all the tombs were interlinked and they chose these four rooms as the setting for their elaborate charade, mixing and matching some of the relics to suit their purposes.

Regardless who the portrait on the middle coffin was of, it has become the image which most people associate with Tutankhamun. As Graham Phillips points out in his book *Act of God – Moses, Tutankhamun and the Myth of Atlantis*, 'We find it reproduced in photographs to promote all manner of Egypt related material: posters to publicize books, brochures to advertise Egyptian holidays, and literature to support Egyptian exhibitions.' Phillips believes the reason for this is that the middle coffin's image is the most lifelike and flattering and shows more of the king's body than the death mask. 'It is altogether a more marketable face,' he explains, 'far more handsome and regal than the chubby youth depicted on the outer coffin, or the innocent child depicted on the inner coffin and the death mask ... the cheekbones were more pronounced, the jaw was firmer and broader, the lips were less full, and the nose was not so long.'[22]

As Carter and his team exposed the final coffin they discovered that the end had been sawn off in order to allow the lid to close. There were even wood shavings, presumably from this job, lying at the bottom of the coffin. Carter would have us believe that this was the work of the people burying the king, but once again it seems unlikely that those entrusted with the burying of a god would behave like this. It is more probably further evidence of the work of Carter's cohorts from Qurna in the years leading up to 1922.

At last the ultimate moment of the search had arrived and it was time to lift the last lid and see what secrets were inside. As the solid gold coffin opened Carter finally came face to face with the mummy of the king, bound in gold and inlay, shining brightly against the dark linens and wearing a life-sized gold mask. 'Time', wrote Carter, 'measured by the brevity of human life, seemed to lose its common perspectives before a spectacle so vividly recalling the solemn religious rites of a vanished civilisation'.[23]

The radiantly handsome mask, weighing over ten kilograms, wore a calm and sad expression. A corselet of gold and inlay bore the inscriptions:

> I reckon your beauties, O Osiris, King Nebkheperura,
> Your soul lives! Your veins are firm!
> Your stability is in the mouth of the living,
> O Osiris, King Tutankhamun.
> Your heart is in your body eternal.[24]

Carter described the funerary mask.

> The beaten golden mask, a beautiful and unique specimen of
> ancient portraiture ... Upon its forehead, wrought in massive
> gold, were the royal insignia – the Nekhebet vulture and Buto
> serpent – emblems of the two kingdoms over which he reigned.
> To the chin was attached the conventional Osiride beard,
> wrought in gold and lapis-lazuli coloured glass; around the
> throat was a triple necklace of yellow and red gold and blue
> faience disk-shaped beads.[25]

Carter's team of experts then had to make their way with scalpels
cautiously through the thirteen layers of rotted linen which bound
the body, revealing yet more golden treasures in each layer. In the
end they found 143 pieces of jewellery, ornaments, amulets and
implements which had been wrapped within the mummy.

Finally they reached the shrunken body of the murdered boy,
naked apart from golden sheaths on his fingers, toes and erect penis.
He was indeed the 'little king', his body measuring less than five feet
five. Carter gently lifted the head and dusted the last few fragments
of decayed linen from it with fine sable brushes to reveal the
handsome features of the Son of God. Carter wrote:

> The youthful Pharaoh was before us at last. An obscure and
> ephemeral ruler, ceasing to be the mere shadow of a name,
> had re-entered, after more than three thousand years, the
> world of reality and history! Here was the climax of our long
> researches! The tomb had yielded its secret: the message of the
> past had reached the present in spite of the weight of time, and
> the erosion of so many years.[26]

The greatest show on earth had reached its climax, a glorious finale combining a staggering display of ancient wealth with the unveiling of timeless mysteries. The world was as enthralled as Carter had intended it to be. He announced that he would rewrap the body and return it to the first gilded coffin to lie in state.

In 1968 the coffin was reopened by R. G. Harrison, professor of anatomy at the University of Liverpool, in order to X-ray the remains to try to determine once and for all the cause of death. Harrison was shocked to discover that Carter had not rewrapped the king as he had claimed, but that Tutankhamun was lying in the same sand tray in which he had been presented to the world through the photographs of Harry Burton. When Harrison brushed aside the sand he discovered that the skull was separated from the first vertebra, and that the arms had been separated at the shoulders, the elbows and the wrists. The legs had also been separated at the hip, knee and ankle joints. The sternum and frontal rib cage were both missing.[27]

Harrison also noticed that the boy's penis was now missing. One can only wonder which private collection houses that ghoulish and undignified relic of ancient history.[28]

The Egyptology establishment chose to ignore Professor Harrison's discovery and you will find little mention of him in any of the books written during the 1970s, when the glorious Tutankhamun exhibition was touring the world. The one exception is the work of Dr Maurice Bucaille, a Frenchman who wrote a book called *Mummies of the Pharaohs*, in which he claimed that Carter 'exaggerated the damage to the outermost wrapping [of the mummy] by asserting in all of his writings that the wrappings and, by a false extension, the mummy itself, had spontaneously suffered from the attack of fatty acids supposedly contained in the ointments poured onto the wrappings [in antiquity] . . .'[29] Bucaille suggested that the damage was actually caused by Carter exposing the corpse to the sun in an unsuccessful attempt to melt the pitch-like material which cemented the body and mask to the base of the coffin.[30]

According to Bucaille, Carter then had to unwrap Tutankhamun and separate the charred, cracked pelvis and lower limbs from the body trunk, so that the jewels and funerary objects could be removed. The head was severed so that it could be left in the coffin while the trunk was removed.[31] In Burton's photographs the top half of the right ear of the corpse also seems to have disappeared without trace.[32] Did it come off with the wrapping and was it simply thrown away? In later pictures the whole ear seems to have gone.

At the time of the discovery these deficiencies seem to have been ignored. Everyone wanted the story to end happily and so, superficially, it did. In due course the bulk of the treasures were extracted from the tomb, packed and transported, with minimal loss, to the Cairo Museum. Pierre Lacau had recognized that the elements of Carter's character which made him such an impossible opponent – his pedantry and stubbornness – equipped him perfectly for the task in hand. If truth be told, clearing the tomb was a job no one else wanted. Destined to take a strenuous decade of Carter's life to complete, it would ultimately be the death of him.

When things were at their most difficult in Egypt, Carter travelled to America on a lecture tour although he first gave the lectures in London at a theatre in Oxford Street. His friends feared that Carter would be ill-equipped to please an audience with his taciturn nature and love of detail, but they had underestimated the showman in him. Audiences hung on his every word. Despite the fact that he had always been a bad communicator and disliked crowds, he was an enormous success. All his latent theatrical skills came to the fore as he relived the story of the discovery which he had invented, along with Carnarvon, in 1922. Audiences would listen spellbound as he described the imaginary moment when he, Carnarvon, Lady Evelyn and Pecky Callender had first peeked through the hole at the treasures beyond. Sometimes he would be so moved by his own story his voice would crack and his eyes would film over. This was a man who had been acting the part for so long he may even have believed his own story. The great and the good flocked to hear him. In America he gave a private talk at the White House to President Calvin Coolidge and in Detroit Henry Ford was one of the audience.[33]

The conservation work in the Valley of the Kings was eventually completed in 1932, a full ten years after the tomb of Tutankhamun had been initially discovered. What was Carter to do now? With his friend, the writer Percy White, he completed the third edition of the immense *The Tomb of Tut-Ankh-Amen*, and began to put together another definitive report on the discovery. He maintained a home on the Theban West Bank but spent most of his time 'sitting in the foyer' of the Winter Palace Hotel in Luxor apparently, according to some, 'sunk in gloom and talking to no one.'[34] Carter later announced that he intended to search for the lost tomb of Alexander the Great. He was convinced that it was located in the environs of Alexandria, Egypt's northern port founded and named after Alexander himself. He maintained that he knew where the tomb was hidden but said, 'I shall not tell anyone about it, least of all the Antiquities Department. The secret will die with me.' And it did.[35] For the next six years he suffered in great anguish, although he still managed to make some visits to his beloved Egypt.

Despite his worldly success and despite the fact that he had grown rich beyond his wildest dreams, Carter died at his Kensington home beside the Albert Hall in 1939, a bitter and relatively obscure man. He never received the knighthood he had so coveted, in spite of the fact that he had made the greatest archaeological find in history. By that time his deception must have been known to many within archaeological and establishment circles. George V, who had died just three years before, had known that Carter and Carnarvon were lying about not entering the Burial Chamber because Carnarvon had let the cat out of the bag during an audience with the king soon after the discovery.

Carter must have lived out his last years in some fear, knowing that many of the people who shared the secrets of the tomb with him had somehow ended up dead in mysterious circumstances. In dark moments he must have thought that it could only be a matter of time before whoever had killed his friends and colleagues came for him. After his death his possessions were auctioned at Sotheby's and the bulk of his modest but exquisite collection of antiquities passed, via King Farouk, to the Cairo Museum. Other pieces were sold privately by the London dealers, Spink, and ended up in a variety of private collections. The Museum of Metropolitan Art took over the house he had lived in during his years in the valley – nicknamed Castle Carter – at Elwat el-Diban.

He went to the grave carrying secrets which we are only just beginning to guess at.

11

THE MISSING PAPYRI

Carter rapidly lost control of himself. One hot word followed
another, until Carter finally abandoned all reserve . . . exclaiming
that unless he received complete satisfaction – 'and justice' – he
would publish, throughout the world, documents contained
in unrevealed papyri he had found in the tomb . . .[1]
Thomas Hoving, *Tutankhamun: The Untold Story*

So what were the secrets which Carter and his friends carried with
them to their graves?

In the dispatch which appeared in *The Times* after the official
opening of the tomb, was a small statement to which no one has
ever attached much weight. The statement claimed that 'important
papyri' as well as historical documents had been found in the tomb
and that they were intact. These documents were immediately
suppressed and have never been seen by anyone again. I believe
they contain information which led to a string of murders. It is
information which is still being suppressed today.

Papyrus was an expensive type of paper, made from a reed of the
same name, which was used by the ancient Egyptians for important
documents. Most tombs contained at least some papyri with official
details of the incumbent recorded on them and some history of the

times that he or she lived in. Over the years of tomb exploration they have been a valuable source of research for historians and academics.

One mention of the Tutankhamun papyri could have been put down to a simple misunderstanding, maybe even an error on the part of a copy-taker or telegraph boy at *The Times*, but that was not the only time that these scrolls were alluded to by those who were in a position to know of their existence.

When the tomb was first opened, Carter and Carnarvon approached a number of experts for help in the clearance process. 'While in Cairo I had time to take stock of the position,' Carter wrote, after the initial burst of euphoria at the discovery. 'And it became more and more clear to me that assistance – and that on a big scale – was necessary if the work in the tomb was to be carried out in a satisfactory manner. The question was, where to turn for this assistance.'[2] One of the people he turned to was Professor James Breasted, the American founder and director of the Oriental Institute of the University of Chicago, an expert in deciphering hieroglyphs and translating the ancient Egyptian language. Carter summoned him to Luxor in order to study these 'important papyri'.[3]

On his arrival however, Breasted was told that an error had been made and the items which had been mistaken for papyri were, in fact, simply bed linens and undergarments belonging to the king which, in the gloom of the tomb, had been mistaken for papyri. That was the last the public ever heard of any papyri, or indeed any records in the tomb at all. However, it seems inconceivable that someone of Carter's experience and methodical nature would have called for Breasted without ascertaining whether the objects he needed help with were written on or not. Travel and communication at the time were awkward and time-consuming affairs, not undertaken without considerable planning and care. Besides which, the thought of Carter mistaking bed linen and undergarments for papyri is ludicrous.[4]

The idea that there would be no written records in a collection so remarkably complete as the one found around the corpse of Tutankhamun is also hard to swallow. There were almost always papyri in the tombs discovered in modern times, even those previously ransacked, because the ancient robbers would have had no interest in them; papyri would have been of no financial value and probably indecipherable. It therefore seems reasonable to assume that there were papyri in the tomb. So why would that fact have to be hushed up? The only explanation I can think of is that whatever Carter, who understood hieroglyphics to a reasonable standard, read in them while waiting for the arrival of Breasted, made him decide to suppress the papyri he had discovered, but that by that time it was too late to stop Breasted. In those days someone in transit would be almost impossible to contact should there be a sudden change of plan.

The dispatch in *The Times* wasn't the only mention of the existence of some mysterious papyri. Upon announcing the discovery, Carnarvon wrote to a friend of his, Wallis Budge, the flamboyant museum collector, saying that they had found papers that would 'change the thinking of the world'.[5] Carnarvon too fell silent on the subject from that moment onwards.

The clinching evidence that there were documents which were never released comes from the mouth of Carter himself. Towards the end of his time in Egypt Carter became infuriated by the lack of support he was receiving from his own government over the division of rewards from the find. He had been trying to arrange an appointment with Lord Allenby, the British High Commissioner, and failing. Running out of patience, he stormed down to the British Embassy in person to give them a piece of his mind. Allenby was unavailable but the furious Carter was finally shown into the office of the Vice Consul. By then he was boiling with indignation and ready to pick a fight with anyone. Someone else at the meeting later described Carter as being 'in a quarrelsome and cantankerous' mood.[6]

As we have seen, diplomatic relations between the British and Egyptian governments were often extremely fraught during this period of growing nationalism within the country. There was also the growing controversy over the establishment of a Palestinian homeland for the Jews. The last thing British officials wanted was a bull like Carter charging around their diplomatic china shop. The Vice Consul, probably irritated by Carter's attitude, told him that they could not be of any assistance to him in what was, when all was said and done, a personal grievance. They argued and Carter's mood grew worse, until eventually he lost the ability to control himself or his tongue any longer. He insulted the competence of the Service of Antiquities and Vice Consul himself.

'Unless I receive complete satisfaction,' he is reported to have roared, 'and justice. I will publish throughout the world, documents from the papyri which I found in the tomb. Documents which will present a true and scandalous account of the exodus of the Jews from Egypt.'[7]

Carter was threatening to stir up trouble between the Jews and the Arabs at a time when everything depended on things remaining calm and the Vice Consul became as furious as Carter. He too lost all his powers of diplomacy and hurled an inkwell at the archaeologist's head. Carter apparently dodged the missile and other people at the meeting came forward to hold the two men apart, but it was too late. The truth had been allowed to slip out in a moment of rage and has remained hanging in the air ever since.

This conversation between Carter and the Vice Consul has never been a secret and has been reported in a number of other books on the subject. (Thomas Hoving found it in notes made by Lee Keedick, who organized Carter's American tour.) Yet no one has yet taken Carter's remarks any further. In his book, *Tutankhamun: The Untold Story*, Thomas Hoving comes to the conclusion that Carter was merely bluffing, trying to intimidate an official who was proving infuriatingly stubborn.[8] If that is the case then it was an extraordinary bluff to choose. How would anyone come up with such a story in the heat of the moment? And why had Carnarvon made a similarly dramatic claim to Wallis Budge several years earlier? I simply don't believe it.

We can be certain that there were some scrolls found in the tomb and they bore some relevance to the Jewish exodus from Egypt. The true identity of the young pharaoh, his father and mother and his lineage would have been spelled out in the papyri which would have been hidden in the kilts of the two sentinels standing outside the Burial Chamber in the Antechamber. That is what such kilts were designed for. In one of his books, *The Tomb of Tut-Ankh-Amen* Carter wrote that by the middle of February 1923 his work clearing the Antechamber was finished, 'with the exception of the two sentinel statues, left for a special reason'.[9] Everything else had been removed to the laboratory and every inch of the floor had been swept and sifted for the last bead or fallen piece of inlay. The 'special reason' for leaving the sentinel statues in place is never given, nor, it seems, has anyone ventured to ask. The most probable reason would have been that their triangular skirts had been opened from the underside, the papyri removed and the skirts resealed with gesso. The results of this action can be seen quite readily by anyone who views the statues today, and Carter therefore wanted to avoid examination of the sentinels by outsiders for as long as possible.

I believe that the writing on the papyri told Carter that the tomb they had stumbled upon was the last resting place of the Son of God. I further believe that the stories of the Bible, including the virgin birth, were actually based on writings about the Egyptian pharaonic family, and we can only speculate as to what other secrets there were in the papyri.

Whatever the details of the revelations, Carter would have realized just how devastating they would be as he perused the papyri. He would certainly have shared the news with his partner in crime, Carnarvon – which was how Carnarvon knew to tell Wallis Budge – and perhaps with the rest of the team as well, or at least some of them.

There is no doubt in my mind that the papyri would have confirmed that Akhenaten was Tutankhamun's father. Perhaps they also confirmed that his mother was Nefertiti, the Egyptian name for Miriam.[10] The scrolls would also have contained details about the religious battles of the time. Akhenaten was a highly controversial figure because he believed there was only one god. This god emanated from the sun and was the unseen god in all things. Akhenaten called him 'The Aten'.

Tutankhamun's great-grandfather was a man called Yuya, who was first identified as the biblical Joseph by Ahmed Osman in *Stranger in the Valley of the Kings.* Osman showed that the chronology of Joseph's life pointed to him serving the Pharaoh Amenhotep II, as did Yuya. In addition to the similarities of their names, in the Bible the pharaoh makes Joseph Master of the Chariots, while

Amenhotep II made Yuya Master of the Horse, for the first time separating the chariots from the rest of the army. Yuya's daughter Tiye married Amenhotep III and was the mother of Akhenaten. Tutankhamun's other biblical ancestors, through his grandmother Tiye, included Abraham and his wife Sarah.[11]

We know for sure that Akhenaten, Tutankhamun's father, was hated by the priests of the time, who could not countenance the fact that he was born from the matriarchal line of a Semitic woman. But he built his own capital at Akhetaten, far away from the Amun priesthood, who were thirsting for his blood, and for a while he lived contentedly with his family. To the Atenists the Pharaoh Akhenaten was God on earth, the physical manifestation of power, who ruled the universe under the sun. But the Egyptian priests had great difficulty in accepting this; they wanted a return to the old ways of worshipping a pantheon of gods, so they forced Akhenaten to abdicate in favour of his son. Certainly if you look at the throne found inside the tomb of Maya, Tutankhamun's wet nurse, you find an interesting picture. The young king is found sitting on the lap of his nurse and behind them are six of his ministers. Five of them are generals – and four of them (Ay, Horemheb, Ramesses I and Seti) followed the young king on the throne. It clearly indicates that Tutankhamun was put on the throne by force. At the same time there is no evidence that Akhenaten was killed in the coup or that he was buried in Egypt. I believe that Akhenaten – the creator of the first monotheistic religion – was Moses, as Ahmed Osman states in his book, *Stranger in the Valley of the Kings*, and that he was driven with the Semites out of Egypt. Petrie found evidence in an Egyptian tomb in Sinai that the Aten religion was worshipped here after it was forbidden in Egypt. One of the artefacts he found was the head of Tiye, Akhenaten's mother.[12]

Tutankhamun, now pharaoh of Egypt, under the tutelage of his uncle Ay, ruled well in spite of the machinations of the ambitious General Horemheb, who saw the boy as the only obstacle in his path to the throne and set about overthrowing him. As Osman shows in *The House of the Messiah*, as Tutankhamun grew older he too returned to the Aten, the religion of his father. His throne depicts him being anointed, under the sun symbol of Aten, as the one true God. Accepting that the concept of one god was too difficult for the ordinary people, he reinstated the old gods as mediators with God (precursors of the angels). In doing so he offended not only the priests of Amun, but the high priest of the new religion.[15]

The evidence for what happens next is to be found in the Bible. St John's gospel says that Moses announced he would be followed by a prophet called Jesus. In the Book of Numbers, it is said that Joshua would follow Moses. Osman argues that Jesus and Joshua are one and the same – and that both are Tutankhamun. There are further parallels. During the time of Moses, his priest Phinhas killed a man who supposedly defiled the temple by hanging him on a tree. The high priest of Aten who was so offended by Tutankhamun's actions was called Pa-nehisi (the Egyptian equivalent of Phinhas). And Tutankhamun himself was killed, as we have seen, and his injury is consistent with hanging. Osman believes that Tutankhamun went to Sinai to see his father and was murdered by the high priest of Aten.[14]

This, I believe, was the story which Carter found himself reading. We can only imagine how the enormity of what they had discovered must have dawned on the explorers: they held in their hands information which could change the thinking of the whole western world and would prove Moses was in fact an Egyptian pharaoh and the Bible based on Egyptian stories. If Carter had been horrified by the amount of attention he had received as one of the discoverers of the tomb, he must have realized that was nothing compared to what would happen if the information contained in the papyri leaked out: the wrath of virtually every political and religious leader in the world would fall on their heads.

It is possible that they toyed with the idea of selling the papyri to the highest bidder; or perhaps decided to conceal them, pretend they never existed. Maybe they did find someone who was willing to buy the scrolls and undertake to ensure the information never leaked out. It is likely there was dissent between Carter and Carnarvon over what they should do.

Whatever their contents, the disappearance of the papyri is to my mind the greatest crime associated with the tomb of Tutankhamun. I have given my reasons for believing that the vast majority of the tomb's contents were secretly plundered with the active or passive connivance of all concerned in the clearing operation. Although it was spectacular and reprehensible, such a robbery was totally human. But, by suppressing the contents of the papyri, that small band of gentlemen thieves condemned many millions to die in needless religious conflicts over the following decades.

Right from the announcement of Carter and Carnarvon's discovery people speculated as to what might truly be happening in the valley, and some came close to working out the truth. On 20 March 1923, a couple of weeks after Carnarvon died, H. V. Morton wrote an article in the *Daily Express* under the headline – 'Lord Carnarvon Poisoned – Is Pharaoh at Work?' 'The real question for us Bible students,' he wrote, 'was whether either of the Pharaohs Akhenaten or Tutankhamun was the spiritual father of Moses.'[15] This suggestion led to assorted rural vicars writing in to discuss whether the evidence contained in the tomb fitted in well with the Bible story including whether Moses was dead long before Tutankhamun was born. They wanted to know which dates were correct, the ones in the Bible or the Egyptian ones, since there was a discrepancy of 150 years. Morton asked in his article why everyone was confusing Akhenaten with Tutankhamun.

On 23 October 1923, Arthur Weigall added to the commotion by announcing to the American public, while on a lecture tour, that, 'It is probable that the opening of the inner tomb will reveal Tutankahmun was the Pharaoh of the Exodus and clear up many obscure points in biblical lore. It also may show that the Jews were migrating to Palestine from Egypt and met Moses and said, "Come on, let's go into this good trade territory in the East." I rather think it may be something interesting like that. Jolly interesting if it were.'[16]

A later convert to the theory that Moses and Akhenaten might be the same man was Sigmund Freud. Although Freud had never actually visited Egypt he had a great affinity for ancient peoples. His guiding maxim in life was always to seek and dispense truth, echoing the ancient pharaonic concept of 'Maat' – total truth. This concept was shown in tomb paintings by the human heart being weighed on the scales of justice by Anubis, the jackal god of the dead, against a feather. Anyone who believes wholeheartedly in the need to seek and dispense the truth is bound to become an embarrassment to someone.

Freud's downfall started in 1901 when, as a forty-five-year-old, he travelled to Rome and saw, for the first time, Michelangelo's statue of Moses. He called this the 'high point of my life', but it wasn't until thirteen years later, just before the outbreak of the Great War, that he wrote in his paper on the 'Moses of Michelangelo' just how much the statue meant to him and how much it pervaded his thoughts. Whenever he found the opportunity he travelled to Rome to see the statue again. He studied it and thought about it incessantly. He said later, 'In 1913, through three lonely September weeks, I stood daily in the church in front of the statue, studied it, measured it, drew it, until that understanding came to me that I only dared to express anonymously in the paper.'[17] I firmly believe that this was when Freud began 'thinking the unthinkable', as he put it, that Moses was a prince or leader in the Egyptian hierarchy. It was a belief which was to lead to his murder.

The final row between Carter and Carnarvon remains something of a mystery. At the beginning of 1923 the tensions in Egypt were building with the heat, which was sometimes averaging over a hundred degrees Fahrenheit in the laboratory, the air outside thick with clouds of dust. Carnarvon was coming under increasing pressure from the Egyptian press and, although he managed to ignore the media most of the time in true patrician style, he was unable to avoid reading some of it. The Egyptian journalists wanted to know what Carnarvon intended to do with 'their mummy'. Carnarvon's temper grew worse and worse until he started falling out with his friends as well as his critics, including Carter. The details have never been revealed, although it is thought the main areas of contention were Carnarvon's handling of the press and the negotiations with the Antiquities Service. There is no doubt that there were some bitter rows, which resulted in Carter ordering Carnarvon from his house, an extraordinary step for the archaeologist who owed everything to his partner to take.[18] It is believed that the two men never saw or spoke to one another again although Carnarvon did send Carter the following letter of apology:

My Dear Carter,

I have been feeling very unhappy today and I did not know what to think or do and then I saw Eve and she told me everything. I have no doubt that I have done many foolish things and I am very sorry. I suppose the fuss and worry have affected me but there is only one thing I want to say to you which I hope you will always remember – whatever your feelings are or will be for me in the future my affection for you will never change.

I'm a man with few friends and whatever happens nothing will ever alter my feelings for you. There is always so much noise and lack of quiet and privacy in the Valley that I felt I should never see you alone although I should like to very much and have a good talk. Because of that I could not rest until I had written to you.

Yours, Carnarvon[19]

What it was that Eve (Lady Evelyn) told him that made him see things differently we will almost certainly never know, although there has been speculation that Carnarvon's daughter developed a crush on Carter. Even if that were true, it seems doubtful that two men of the world with so many other things on their minds, would have fallen out over such a matter. Something far more fundamental must have come between them.

In 1997, with nearly all the material for this book in place, I decided to make one more trip to the valley; I wanted, if at all possible, to get inside the Burial Chamber, which is kept out of bounds to visitors with a padlocked door, allowing them to look in at the solitary corpse from a viewing platform where Carter's partition wall once stood.

A friend who was leaving for Egypt before me agreed to contact the Director General of Antiquities in Upper Egypt, Dr Muhammed El Saghir, to see if I could get permission to film in the Burial Chamber. When I arrived at his office, El Saghir was talking to a gentleman on the other side of the room. He introduced me to his friend, who he called Ahmed. Only later did I discover that Ahmed was actually Dr Muhammed Nasr, Director General of Antiquities at Qurna. I was invited to have coffee and proceeded to tell them what I wanted. I talked of my suspicions, of who I thought the body was and said that I believed Carnarvon and Carter had been plundering the tomb for years before they pretended to discover it for the first time. None of this seemed to surprise them, but the story of the missing papyri and the subsequent murders gave them cause for thought.

'Well, Mr O'Farrell,' Ahmed said. 'Where do you think these papyri are now?'

'I don't have the remotest idea,' I replied, 'or even if they still exist. I suspect a copy of them is either buried under Castle Carter in the valley, or with Carter in Putney Cemetery. I feel sure that a man as meticulous as Carter would have made copies of them, so they may be in several places.'

'When can Mr O'Farrell visit the tomb?' Ahmed asked Dr El Saghir.

'He can go with you today,' he replied.

The only time to be really alone in the valley is during the lunch break between 12.00 and 1.30. Since it was already eleven o'clock I arranged to meet Ahmed the next day in his office at the foot of the valley.

Not surprisingly, given my excitement, I was early for the appointment and waited in the café at the entrance to the valley. At exactly half past eleven a guide collected me and escorted me to meet Ahmed and another colleague. We walked the short distance to the tomb in the burning midday heat, talking and joking as we went.

The steps down to the tomb were white and new-looking and the passageway was scattered with the clean white chips which I believe are part of the detritus from Carter's work. Inside the Antechamber Ahmed climbed over the viewing parapet and stood by the pharaoh's tomb. I asked if I could follow and one of the guards unlocked the little padlocked door to the tomb for me. Ahmed gestured to two red roses lying by the king's bier. 'A beautiful young French lady dropped them earlier this morning,' he explained.

It seemed a sensitive gesture and I photographed them. The next moment I was through the door. Ahmed pointed out that I was standing on the top of the king's sarcophagus lid, which was on the floor covered by a thick clear plastic sheet to protect it from desecrators like myself. I hastily hopped off. I could see the crack across the top quite clearly. It seemed obvious to me that this lid could never have been intended for the beautiful tomb. I took pictures of the inner walls and of the tomb itself, explaining to my new friend where I thought the entries and exits to the tomb had taken place. Ahmed asked me to show him where I thought the long corridor leading from the tomb of Ramesses VI was which I did.

Far too soon we were back out in the dazzling light.

'Do you know where the cache that Theodore Davis found was?' Ahmed asked me. We walked across and he told me that he thought it could link with the king's grave. I told him I thought the same thing. I had a feeling he knew much more than he was saying, listening to me and mentally matching the information with whatever he already knew. Davis's shallow pit lies exposed, supposedly of no importance now that it has been emptied. I believe that were anyone to restart digging there they would soon find that it is part of the subterranean complex leading to Tutankhamun's tomb. Professor Nicholas Reeves did just that earlier last year – the results are not yet published.

Standing in the silent heat of the barren valley it is hard to imagine just what dramas and passions have been acted out here over the millennia. The most recent of them, I believe, was the triggering of the string of murders in the first half of the twentieth century which have become known as the 'mummy's curse'.

12

A STRING OF NECESSARY MURDERS

Osiris . . . Great is the awe of him in the hearts of men,
spirits and the dead . . . and many are his shapes in the Pure Place.[1]
Book of the Dead

I don't know whether someone within the British establishment deliberately decided that they would foster the idea of the mummy's curse, or whether it was simply their good fortune that the rumours arose when they did. What I do know is that the stories of an ancient spell provided a useful cover for a string of murders carried out over a number of years to ensure that the secrets of the hidden papyri were never revealed.

Carnarvon was the first one whose death was attributed to the curse, although possibly not the first to be murdered by the authorities who wished to hush up the existence of the papyri. I suspect that he was poisoned; it has been reported that he was mummified immediately after his death, his viscera being removed in a hospital in Cairo.[2] This occurred in spite of the fact that in his will he stipulated that 'Two doctors be in attendance to ensure that I am actually dead.'[3]

If someone has been murdered with the use of poison, it would be sensible for the killers to remove the stomach, which would contain the evidence, as quickly as possible.

His wife, Almina, flew from England to be by her husband's side when she heard how ill he was, but wasn't in as much of a hurry as one might expect under the circumstances. She apparently took ill after flying across the English Channel and put down at Paris' Le Bourget airfield. Almina made the rest of the journey to Cairo by boat from Marseilles, hardly the route of a woman in a hurry to see her husband before he died. Perhaps she had been advised to delay her arrival as death, though imminent, had not yet laid its grisly hand on the English lord and arrangements to finally ease the earl out of the land of the living had not yet been completed. By that stage their marriage was an unhappy affair, as evidenced by the fact that a few months after Carnarvon's death, the forty-seven-year-old widowed countess flew on down to South Africa and married her lover, Lieutenant Colonel Ian Orislow Dennistoun, a divorcee four years her junior who had been in the Grenadier Guards.[4]

Upon his death, Carnarvon's permit to dig was inherited by Almina. She also inherited the Carnarvon collection at Highclere, which by then consisted of 1,218 objects or groups of objects, nearly all of which had been acquired for him by Carter, working on commission. In his will, as Nicholas Reeves states, Carnarvon suggested that Almina, 'should she find it necessary to sell ... I suggest that the nation [the British Museum] be given first refusal at £20,000, far below its value.' If the British Museum turned the offer down, Carnarvon continued, 'I would suggest that the collection be offered to the Metropolitan, New York, Mr Carter to have charge of the negotiations and to fix the price.'[5]

Almina decided she did want to sell but wasn't too keen on the idea of letting the British Museum have the collection at such a good price. She was however obliged to abide by the letter of her late husband's will. So she and Carter devised a plan, further evidence of Carter's devious ingenuity. The British Museum was asked whether it would like to buy the collection for £20,000. If they did, then they would have to pay for it by four that afternoon. Not surprisingly, the museum was unable to meet the deadline and Almina, her conscience clear, sold the collection to the Metropolitan for $145,000 (around £30,000), half as much again more than the British Museum would have been obliged to pay.[6]

Carnarvon, who had already been indiscreet to one or two people, such as Wallis Budge, about the papyri was obviously the one the establishment wanted to silence first. But then there were others: people who Carnarvon or Carter might have talked to about the find and who were likely to expose the secret. Plans must have been laid from that moment on, although the killings were going to need to be spaced out if they were to avoid attracting so much suspicion that the police would be forced to investigate.

Several of the deaths attributed to the curse, like the small boy who fell under the wheels of a hearse, can be discounted as unfortunate coincidence, but the ones involving the people who would have had knowledge of the contents of the tomb seem to form an eerie pattern. One of the most significant fatalities was that of Baron Richard Bethel who was secretary and confidant to Carnarvon in the months leading up to the earl's death. It is highly likely that he knew a great deal about the papyri. Carnarvon would have felt completely comfortable with a fellow aristocrat and the two of them must have spent a great deal of time together while travelling. It seems inevitable that they would have talked about everything under the sun, including the intriguing contents of the papyri. Bethel died under mysterious circumstances in his London club. Supposedly dying in his sleep of a coronary thrombosis, his death is quite consistent with a pillow being placed over his mouth, smothering him.

Three months later, Bethel's father Lord Westbury, also died, a supposed suicide. Although he was an old man, the manner of his death was highly suspicious and it seems more than likely that if Bethel was going to confide what he knew about the papyri, his father would be one of the people he would talk to. *The Times*, on 22 February 1930, printed a column-long report of the coroner's inquest which was careful not to ask too many difficult questions.

The main witness was Westbury's night nurse. She had been looking after him for some ten weeks by then. She told the court how at 8.30 p.m. the night before his death, she had administered a dram and a half of bromide and one twenty-fourth of a grain of heroin to her employer to assist him in sleeping. He slept until midnight, at which time he woke and had some barley water, remarking to her that it was too early for his Ovaltine. He went back to sleep until 2.30 a.m. before waking again to have his Ovaltine. She repeated the dose of heroin at three o'clock, before settling him back to sleep.

When he woke again at 7.00 a.m., he appeared to her to be comfortable and drowsy. He asked her the time and had another glass of barley water. The nurse told the court how she shook his pillow and he turned on his side, saying it was too early to finally wake up for the day and telling her to go out of the room and not wake him again until eight.

The nurse then put coal on the fire at about 7.10 a.m. before going to the kitchen to put Westbury's coffee on and see to the milk for breakfast. As she worked she heard a crash of breaking glass and ran back to her patient's room where she found the bed empty and the window, which had previously been closed, hanging open. A washing stand had been moved from in front of the window and the curtain had been dislodged. The nurse ran downstairs at once but, she said, 'They would not let me go further.'

No one questioned her as to who 'they' might be or why they would stop her going to the man she was supposed to be nursing, who was now obviously badly injured.

'Did you know he was likely to commit suicide?' the coroner enquired of the woman.

'No,' she replied. 'He often thought he was ill and that he was going to die, but never anything like that.'

Two letters were then produced which supposedly had been on the washing stand, although the nurse had never seen them before. Both were written on black-edged notepaper, one addressed to 'Dearest George', the other to a Mrs White Forwood, in an envelope addressed to his wife, Lady Westbury. The coroner said that one of the letters read, 'I really cannot stand any more horrors and I hardly see what good I am going to do here. So I am going to make my exit. Goodbye, and if you were right, all will be well. Your affectionate . . .' The rest of the letter was difficult to make out, but he wrote something about a Sister Catherine having a hundred pounds and thanked his housekeeper for her overwhelming kindness. The letter ended up with 'I am off.'

A valet at King's House, two doors away, reported that at roughly 7.25 a.m., as he was going to court, he saw a felt slipper fall into the courtyard at the staff entrance. When he looked up about thirty feet he saw, coming through the air, the body of Lord Westbury. The body turned a complete somersault before hitting the glass canopy. A woman just had time to throw herself clear before being hit. The valet added that Lord Westbury, who was very badly injured and certainly unconscious, just gave a couple of groans and a slight spasmodic heave and was gone within a minute.

The coroner closed the inquest by saying, 'No doubt, poor Lord Westbury has been suffering very much and had difficulty sleeping. He also was old and depressed and lost his son not very long ago.' He recorded a verdict of 'suicide while of unsound mind'.[7]

The fall from the seventh-floor window to the ground was about seventy-two feet. To get out of the window the elderly Lord Westbury would have had to have got over a sill which was two feet three inches wide. Then there was another sill of eight inches and a gutter of two and half feet and a parapet of thirteen inches. A total width of six and a half feet. We are asked to believe that fifteen minutes after the nurse left the room, having been told to come back in an hour, a drowsy Lord Westbury, who had just imbibed a barley water and asked to be allowed to sleep for another forty-five minutes or so, made up his mind to get out of bed, move a washstand and launch himself from the window, flying over a parapet six and a half feet.

And where did the letters come from? Did he write them the night before and only get them out after he had enjoyed his night's sleep and various drinks? Did he dash them off in that quarter of an hour? At what stage did he decide to use black-bordered notepaper for his suicide notes? Why would he go to so much trouble and then allow his writing to become indecipherable at certain stages of the letters? Is it not more likely that someone came in through the window from the wide ledge outside, moved the washstand, pulled back the curtains, threw the elderly lord out of the window (thereby causing the somersault motion that the valet described) and left the letters on the washstand before disappearing.

In her testimony, the nurse claimed that Lord Westbury did not have trouble sleeping unless he had something worrying him, but the coroner contradicted her in his closing remarks. He also led another witness by saying that one of the letters was 'obviously a farewell letter'.[8] Nor did the coroner think to ask why a man planning to jump out of a window would bother to move a wash-stand first. It would not have been difficult for one man to walk round a single piece of furniture to reach the window, but it might have been more difficult for a man, or possibly two, attempting to throw someone else out, someone who might be putting up a struggle, however feeble.

Who was the woman that Lord Westbury nearly fell on and what was she doing there at that hour of the morning? Again, it seems as if nobody asked.

George Jay Gould, the American railroad tycoon and another good friend of Carnarvon's, allegedly died of pneumonia (the cause of death officially attributed to Carnarvon himself) soon after visiting his friend in Egypt and viewing the tomb.[9] Until that moment Gould had been in perfect health and was a keen tennis player. Is it possible that Gould had confided to the wrong people something that Carnarvon had told him on that visit? Or was this just another coincidence?

Another to die unexpectedly was Arthur Weigall, the *Daily Mail* journalist who had followed the happenings of the discovery and clearance so closely and who had been the one to predict that Carnarvon would be dead within six weeks of the Burial Chamber opening. As we have seen, prior to writing for the *Mail*, Weigall had held the same job as Carter in the Antiquities Service for the Egyptian government. Of all the outside observers of the work,

Weigall was the most knowledgeable and the most dangerous to anyone wanting to hide the truth.

He had already linked in print the Exodus with Akhenaten's revolution and believed the Israelites were driven out of Egypt at the end of Tutankhamun's reign by Horemheb, the general who later proclaimed himself pharaoh.[10] According to Weigall, the Israelites were not only implicated in Akhenaten's heresy but may even have caused it.[11] When the old religion of Amun and the other gods was restored at Thebes under Tutankhamun and consolidated under his successors, notably Ay and Horemheb, the Israelites were ill-treated, persecuted, and ultimately 'thrust out of Egypt'. Weigall also wrote: 'I need not point out how wide an area of thought is opened up by this supposition that Moses lived through the Aten heresy. For the question as to what connection there was between the Hebrew monotheism and this earliest known monotheism of the Egyptians will at once present itself to the reader.'[12]

Weigall was a fervent believer in telling the truth at all times. It is obvious from his writings that he had figured out just who Tutankhamun really was. Had he eventually written down everything that he knew and suspected, he would have been highly dangerous to anyone who wanted to conceal the truth; he had to be removed.

Georges Benédite, the French head of archaeology in Cairo claimed that the tomb was not Tutankhamun's; he fell to his death down a flight of steps.[13]

Arthur Mace, who had been with Carter from the very beginning of the adventure and who must have been privy to any concealments, was also sacrificed on the wheel of necessity, dying in a manner which is, once again, consistent with poisoning. In a period of seven years, between the deaths of Carnarvon and Westbury, eight people who had knowledge of what had really transpired in the tomb had been eliminated. But the most knowledgeable was still alive.

The reason Carter lasted as long as he did may have had something to do with his personality. He was not a 'clubbable' man. It is unlikely that he ever indulged in gossip in the same way as men like Carnarvon and Bethel would have done. He simply didn't have a wide or influential enough social circle to be an immediate danger, nor was he as likely to be believed by the people who mattered. His dispatch was, perhaps, deemed less urgent than the others. Carter did not want to tell the world what they had discovered. He did not want to rock the boat. He was like a thief who breaks into a house and finds a dead body there. He wanted to keep everything as quiet as possible.

It seems likely to me, however, that the deaths which were caused by the secrets of the papyri actually continued for a far longer period, and included deaths other than those generally associated with the 'curse'. I believe they started several years before Carnarvon's death and went on for decades afterwards, reaching all the way to Sigmund Freud himself.

13

Did Davis, Ayrton and Jones also know too much?

As we clambered down into the shadows, we saw in the distance a
great motionless cloud of dust, and in the stillness heard the rhythmic
minor chant of native workmen singing . . . We soon came upon [Davis]
standing with two or three other gentlemen, looking on with
obvious excitement as his men dug at the entrance-shaft of a tomb
they had discovered only a few hours earlier. He was smoking
cigarette after cigarette, intermittently leaving the group
to pace nervously back and forth . . .[1]

Charles Breasted

Carnarvon's wasn't the first death in suspicious circumstances connected with the tomb. Mysterious things had started happening as far back as 1907, when Theodore Davis became involved with the hunt for Tutankhamun.

Davis first became involved in excavations through Carter who, having not yet met Carnarvon, was in need of someone who could finance his plans. Davis soon became addicted to the thrill of the hunt and they worked together from 1902 to 1904 when Carter transferred to his new job as chief inspector in the north. The following year, Carter's successor James Edward Quibell, unearthed for Davis an incredibly rich tomb containing Yuya and Tjuyu (the biblical Joseph and his wife, the parents of Queen Tiye). This was the best find so far in the valley, and must have caused Carter enormous chagrin. Davis, now an elderly man, began to treat the whole valley as if it was his personal property.

Quibell was then also transferred to the northern inspectorate and was replaced by Arthur Weigall. The reason given for Quibell's transfer was that Davis was becoming increasingly difficult to control and was riding roughshod over him. Weigall suggested that Davis should hire his own private archaeologist to oversee his workings and report to the chief inspector. The first to take up this post was Edward Ayrton, a young man of twenty-three with apparently boundless energy but some unfortunate characteristics.[2]

'Ayrton . . . was not popular at night,' wrote Joseph Lindon Smith. 'By consensus, his cot was placed a long distance away from the rest of us. He had dreadful nightmares in which he shrieked in fluent Chinese . . .'[3]

Davis had him commence excavating in the West Valley near the tomb of Amenophis III, which had been discovered by Napoleon's men in 1799. After a desultory start, Ayrton gave it up and was sent instead to the rich and more promising East Valley, to dig around an earlier tomb, KV12. Less than a year later the French Institute in Cairo took over where Ayrton had left off in the West Valley. It is hard to understand how they could do this when Davis had the concession, unless Davis allowed it. Perhaps Davis had found out what he had long suspected, and so no longer needed to dig in the West Valley. Carter and Carnarvon had often boasted of pulling the wool over the eyes of the 'stupid American',[4] but maybe Davis had seen through the pretence and flummery of this Anglo-French club and was using his lawyer's acuity to outwit Carter.

It is possible that Davis suspected that a tunnel linked the tomb of Amenophis III in the West Valley to that of KV12, a tomb which was less than one hundred yards from that of Tutankhamun. Maybe Davis sent Ayrton to excavate at the tomb of Amenophis III and had his suspicions confirmed that a tunnel did exist under the valley ridge, terminating in the vicinity of KV12. If so, he would have known that it would very possibly lead to the tomb of Tutankhamun.

At first Ayrton found nothing at KV12 and moved to the partially explored tomb of Tuthmosis IV and later to nearby KVB. He then excavated at the tomb of Ramesses IV (KV2), about 160 yards from Tutankhamun's tomb. Clearly, Davis had his man looking for Tutankhamun's tomb and eventually Ayrton found it, but was never to know that he had, or was never able to say that he had.

Remarkably, in the vicinity of KV12 Ayrton had uncovered a blue faience cup with Tutankhamun's throne-name inscribed upon it. Davis was now getting closer to his goal of finding the tomb of the young Egyptian king. For Carter, it must have been a worrying time. Ayrton's search then became more methodical, making use of, as he put it, 'the policy of exhausting every mountain and foothill in the Valley.'[5] His efforts were successful for, in the rubble of KV14, he found a box with Horemheb's name upon it, and then a new tomb, Siptah's. From here he progressed to tomb number KV35, again only 160 yards from the entrance to the tomb of Tutankhamun. His final efforts were the uncovering of tomb KV6, only fifty yards away from the greatest find of all.[6]

Then came the great prize of KV55, the tomb of mystery. It contained a dismantled shrine, a collapsed coffin and a mummy. It was identified as the tomb of Queen Tiye, although the beautiful cartonage mask had been ripped in half, making visual identification of the mummy virtually impossible. Davis was completely convinced that he had found the body of Queen Tiye and had two doctors examine the mummy, one of them an American gynaecologist. They agreed that the mummy was that of an old woman.[7]

She was shipped to Cairo for examination by Sir Grafton Elliot Smith, the greatest forensic pathologist of his day, and Davis confidently expected Smith to confirm that the mummy was that of Queen Tiye. Imagine his horror when Smith declared that the mummy he had received was that of a young man, about twenty-three years of age. Smith wrote to Weigall, 'Are you sure that the bones you sent me are those which were found in the tomb? Instead of the bones of an old woman, you have sent me those of a young man. Surely there is some mistake.'[8]

Davis knew the mummy was that of an old woman; he had the testimony of his experts, plus Ernest Jones, who had sketched the body. The mummy Smith had couldn't possibly be the same one he had dispatched. However, a further discovery made during Elliot Smith's examination of the mummy was that the gold vulture band around its brow was not a female crown, as first thought, but the vulture collar of male pharaonic burials. The mistake, it was decided, was due to the fact that the collar had fallen up over the head when the bier collapsed, giving it the appearance of a headdress. The mummy was therefore not only unquestionably male, but also a king.[9]

Eventually, modern forensic techniques enabled a likely relationship to be established between Tutankhamun and the mysterious mummy. In 1966, an examination of the remains established once and for all that the mummy was male and about twenty. It also concluded that he and Tutankhamun shared the same blood group and type; they were almost certainly brothers.[10]

Did Davis, Ayrton and Jones also know too much?

Although no references to a brother of Tutankhamun have been found, there was a man who lived just before the young king's short reign who may have been just that. Carved portraits depict someone called Ankhkheperure with the title Nefernefruaten, 'Fair is the beauty of the (god) Aten', suggesting Ankhkheperure was related to Nefertiti.[11] As she has no recorded male children, then this young man was probably a nephew and therefore could easily have been Tutankhamun's brother. As Graham Phillips suggests in his book *Acts of God, Moses, Tutankhamun and the Myth of Atlantis*, this young man, more generally known as Smenkhkara, was most likely Akhenaten's chosen successor and probably did take the throne for a short time prior to Tutankhamun. If Smenkhkara was the mysterious mummy in tomb 55, as Phillips suggests, then the sealing of the tomb with his successor Tutankhamun's cartouche means that it must have been reopened within a few years of the original interment, which is exactly what the evidence from Tutankhamun's own tomb reveals. Phillips further concludes in his book that there is little doubt that Smenkhkara was the person represented on the middle coffin in Tutankhamun's tomb.[12]

A new theory has emerged recently, which is discussed by my friend and fellow author, Charles Pope, to the effect that the Queen Tiye find had to be hushed up because of some information that came to light in the tomb, probably in some papyri like the ones missing from Tutankhamun's tomb. This theory is even more shocking than the one which equates Akhenaten with Moses. It is that the Greek myth of Oedipus was based on an Egyptian tale which referred to a relationship between Akhenaten and his mother, Queen Tiye.[13]

If there was such an incestuous relationship between these two, which resulted in the births of Smenkhkara and Tutankhamun, then the authorities would most certainly have wanted to keep it quiet. Imagine the shock which would have been caused by the revelation that Akhenaten, Moses and Oedipus were all the same person; that the father of the Jews was in fact a practitioner of incest, and that the virgin birth, which is so much a part of mainstream religion was, in fact, the result of just such a relationship. The Messiah would then not so much be the Son of God as the son of Moses and his grandmother!

So it seems certain that, for whatever reason, someone had switched Queen Tiye's body for that of Smenkhkara in transit. Davis knew he had been duped, but who would ever believe that respectable professionals from the world of archaeology would even contemplate such a plan, let alone execute it? Davis could do nothing but rant and insist that he had discovered the body of Queen Tiye. The more he ranted, and the quieter his opponents remained, the more the world in general assumed he was mistaken in his beliefs.

In a letter to Arthur Weigall, the language scholar A. H. Sayce wrote, 'I am afraid you might as well try to stop an avalanche as to try to stop Mr Davis when he is hell bent on doing a particular thing.'[14] The roar of the Davis 'avalanche' must have been particularly ominous to Carter, who was systematically homing in on his treasure trove but had to watch Davis getting closer and closer. KV62 was just forty yards away from where Davis was now working.

Success followed success for Ayrton and Davis. From KV56 Ayrton brought out a spectacular hoard of jewellery which almost certainly signed both his and Davis's death warrants. It was January 1908 and Carter now had Carnarvon on his team. He was ready to move. In February Ayrton discovered the great gold tomb of Horemheb.

At the pinnacle of his success, Ayrton announced his decision to retire and allow the sick, tubercular Ernest Jones to replace him. At least that was the official story. It seems incredible to me that anyone would make this decision at such a glorious moment and much more likely that he was bribed to withdraw from the work. An offer was made which was too good to refuse, but it was one which was to mean no more than a stay of execution. He left Egypt and joined an archaeological survey in Ceylon. In 1911 he drowned while out on a shooting expedition.[15]

His replacement, Ernest Jones, was a small, pleasant, dark-haired young Welshman who initially signed up with Davis as field director and artist for three months, at a fee of £250, hoping to emulate the success of Ayrton. He and Davis, however, soon proved to be incompatible; Davis was becoming more irascible and Jones's health deteriorated. Despite this, they continued to work together for three years but found little of any real importance. Davis felt that the British archaeologists were 'using him', and this did not help Jones who did, however, discover tomb 58, his greatest find, of which he said, 'The next day we began going down the pit finding very interesting fragments of furniture all thrown about in the debris and of an interesting period – the end of the XVIII dynasty, the objects bearing cartouches of the Pharaoh Aye and of another called Tut-ankh-amon, the latter of whom has not yet been discovered or his tomb ...'

This was in 1909, yet Davis in his work *The Tombs of Harmhabi and Tutankhamun, 1912*, wrote that Ayrton was the discoverer of KV58 in 1907. Although Davis is known for being careless in his writings, this seems a particularly major error of memory. That the one really first-class discovery made by Jones should be credited to Ayrton two years earlier seems highly mysterious.

Jones's health, the accounts claim, grew steadily worse and he died of consumption in 1911. A year before his death he wrote, 'Latterly the work has been very dusty – being very painful and trying for me – I will be very glad when the excavations are over. I really don't feel up to the work and don't know what I shall do next year. I don't feel up to taking it on again – if I live so long.'[16] Maybe it was the tuberculosis that killed him, or maybe he learned something about the mysterious tomb 55 which made him dangerous to the authorities. Davis might have passed on his suspicions about the switched body and Jones would have had a lot of time to think about possible explanations.

Davis must have known that as an American and an outsider, the cards were stacked against him, despite his spectacular run of success. He was an intelligent man and must have known that Carter was simultaneously using him and holding him in contempt.

Jones and Ayrton both died in 1911 and Davis in 1914, which meant that the three people who knew the most about the tombs, apart from Carter, had disappeared within three years. Arthur Weigall wrote:

> Owing to some curious idiosyncrasy of old age, Mr Davis entertained a most violent and obstinate objection to the suggestion that we had discovered the body of Akhenaten. He had hoped that he had found Queen Taia [which he had] and when he was at last forced to abandon this fallacy, he seemed to act almost as though desiring to obscure the identification of the

body. He was still in a passionate state of mind in this regard when, a few years later, his brain gave way and a tragic oblivion descended upon him.[17]

To state that Ayrton, Jones and Davis were murdered by a person or persons unknown is not something to assert lightly in the absence of obvious evidence. There is no 'smoking gun'. We have to look at the circumstantial evidence surrounding these deaths and their relationship to each other. Then we have to look for a motive.

All had worked together in the valley and two of them were trained Egyptologists. Between them they had found more tombs than had ever been found before. Suppose that Carter, while working for Davis in 1904, discovered Tutankhamun's tomb and then resigned for specious reasons. Once Carter had been introduced to Carnarvon, Carter would have appraised his new partner of all he knew about Tutankhamun's whereabouts and between them they put together a master plan to ensure that they did not have to share the find with Davis or the authorities. Ayrton was already proving too successful and the danger was that he would find the tomb before Carter and Carnarvon could get the concession that Davis held; and the game was almost lost when Ayrton found KV55 in 1907.

Carter and Carnarvon would then have been in a quandary. If it was established that the body in KV55 was Queen Tiye, it would only be a matter of time before the energetic Ayrton found Tutankhamun. Drastic action was called for and Carter was not averse to action. If the gold sheets from Tiye's tomb disappeared (and he made sure they did), and then the smashed sarcophagus (which eventually found its way to a museum in Munich, with the gold sheets, where it still resides today),[18] then enough confusion would be caused to throw the identity of the occupant of the tomb into serious doubt.

It was Carter who proposed that both the mummy and the sarcophagus be shipped to Cairo for forensic examination by Smith, who assumed there had been a mistake. There was no mistake; Carter did not operate that way. He must have switched the mummies. It was no wonder that Davis was apoplectic. He realized that it was hopeless to struggle against what he called these 'matters of deceit'.[19] The crisis for Carter and Carnarvon was thus avoided for the moment but Davis, Ayrton and Jones knew the truth and their lips would have to be sealed.

Ayrton's drowning in 1911 was invariably described at the time as accidental. Surely the word is not required, for if it was intended it would have been classed as suicide and, if someone engineered it, murder?

There is no doubt that Jones had been in bad health. In one pathetic letter home he wrote about his sad state. This was a little over a year before Jones's death and the overriding impression from reading the letter is that he was dying, not of tuberculosis but of boredom. There was obviously little to do and Davis must have been increasingly difficult to work for as he would have known full well that he was on an impossible mission.

Even with Jones dead and Ayrton gone from Egypt, Davis was still a big threat to Carter and Carnarvon. He could, and did, hire another archaeologist, and so a man had to be found who would be amenable to Carter and Carnarvon's plans. That man was Harry Burton from the Metropolitan Museum, the institution which was to benefit most from the eventual 'discovery' by Carter and Carnarvon, and the same Burton who said that Davis had found the tomb of

Did Davis, Ayrton and Jones also know too much?

Tutankhamun.[20] Davis, in despair, gave up in 1914 and died a broken man. Like Ayrton and Jones, he knew too much and even though out of Egypt, he could still have thwarted the conspirators. He had to go.

So the so-called 'curse' actually began to strike much earlier than is usually recorded and was to go on much later, encompassing one of the world's most famous names: Sigmund Freud.

14

MOSES, SCROLLS AND THE
MURDER OF SIGMUND FREUD

The Jew is a creation of the man Moses,
who had been an Egyptian Nobleman.[1]
Sigmund Freud

I firmly believe that one of the last victims of the murder plot which
masqueraded as a curse was Sigmund Freud, the father of psycho-
analysis.

Freud wrote a paper entitled 'The Moses of Michelangelo'. The
Michelangelo figure is larger than life, showing Moses as a strong,
vigorous old man. His brow is adorned with symbolic horns, denot-
ing the transfiguration after Moses had seen God. The long beard is
grasped with the left hand and touched with the forefinger of the
right. He is deep in thought as he sits frowning, holding the tablets
of the law.[2] Freud wondered just what it was that Michelangelo was
trying to depict. Was Moses making a decision, or had he already
made one? Was he just seated or about to rise? His leg muscles
suggest action; and what about the tablets of stone? Was he about to
break them in rage over the profanation of his beliefs by his people?[3]

Finally, Freud decided what it was the great artist had been trying
to convey in his sculpture. Unlike those who had interpreted Michelangelo's masterpiece as a man driven beyond endurance; betrayed

by the people he had sought to save and about to smash the tablets of law in a violent fury, Freud postulated that Michelangelo, by the careful placing of the hands on the tablets, was showing that Moses was actually subjugating the rage that had risen in him. He was not about to commit a violent act, but was in fact fighting against his own passion, subduing it and thus rising above his own nature. In Michelangelo's Moses the crisis had passed and the statue represented 'not the introduction of a violent action but the remnants of a terminated movement'.[4]

It would appear that as early as 1923 Freud had realized that something of importance had been uncovered, by Carter and Carnarvon in the tomb of Tutankhamun. He believed whatever it was would offer support to his theory that Moses was, in fact, a high-ranking Egyptian official. The connection between the two was possibly brought to light by the archaeologist Battiscombe Gunn who was present at the official opening of the tomb. Coincidentally, Gunn's wife worked at Freud's clinic in Vienna and it is impossible to doubt that the tomb of Tutankhamun, would not have been talked about at great length. Whether or nor Carter and Freud were in contact with one another, through Gunn, is impossible to ascertain as Freud's personal letters are now held by the Sigmund Freud Archives Inc., New York. The Archive was founded by Dr Kurt Eissler who, almost single-handedly, collected a vast amount of documentation from the time, and personally interviewed a great number of people who had been analyzed by Freud. Regrettably, Dr Eisslers' work is not available for scrutiny. This material is being suppressed in the same way as the writings from the tomb.[5]

Probably the first attempt on Freud's life took place in 1923. Freud, a physician, detected a 'leukoplastic growth on my jaw and palate'.

He was then in his sixty-seventh year. He had the growth removed and was told that it was not cancerous, but it grew back. Freud believed it was malignant. He chose to go to a surgeon called Marcus Hajek, a nose specialist. Freud expressed doubts about Hajek's skills but still entrusted him with the operation, perhaps because he couldn't persuade anyone else to do it.[6]

According to Peter Gay in his biography on Freud, it would appear that Freud's doubts about Hajek were well founded. It later became apparent that Hajek, although a capable surgeon, knew the operation was purely cosmetic and quite uncalled for, but he still carried out the procedure in the out-patient's department of his clinic. The facts regarding what happened next are slightly ambiguous but something definitely went terribly wrong on the operating table causing Freud to bleed profusely. He was taken to a small side room to recover. The other patient in the room, according to Freud's daughter, being a friendly, retarded dwarf. Having been told her father was quite all right, Anna went shopping for him. Meanwhile, Freud began to bleed badly once more and tried to ring the bell for assistance. It did not work. He was too frail to stand or shout for help and it seemed that his life was fading fast. The dwarf, however, ran to get the nurse, who successfully stemmed the bleeding.

Gay also reports that from that moment on Anna refused to leave her father's side and, together with the dwarf, kept vigil over his bed. In the middle of the night Freud's condition deteriorated and Anna called the nurse once more. At once they both attempted to summon the house surgeon but the man refused to come. Thankfully, Freud survived the night despite this quite blatant act of negligence and the next day he was discharged from the hospital.[7]

Had it not been for the efforts of Anna and the dwarf, Freud would have died that night, very painfully. I do not believe it was an accident that the bell did not work nor a coincidence that the surgeon did not come when called. I believe it was a deliberate attempt on the old man's life. If Freud had died it would have looked like an accident, a botched operation to remove a growth gone horribly wrong, nothing more sinister than that. Had the attempt on Freud's life succeeded he would have died the same year as Carnarvon. As it was he struggled on another sixteen years and finally died in the same year as Howard Carter, when he was the victim of a supposed mercy killing by a friend. After the German invasion of Austria, Freud and his daughter escaped to London where he completed his book *Moses and Monotheism*, publishing it against the advice of men like Professor Yehuda and historian Charles Singer, who feared that the book would provoke antisemitism. In London Freud was operated on, at the instigation of his friend and doctor Max Schur, for a cancerous growth near his jaw. In fact, no medical report indicating that the growth removed was cancerous has ever been found. Freud was in considerable pain after the operation, unable to eat and close to death. Max Schur eventually gave him a lethal dose of morphine, persuading Anna that this was what her father wanted.[8] The question remains, why was an old man subjected to such terrible operations?

In the same year that he died, his last book *Moses and Monotheism* was published in New York. Freud described himself as 'thinking the unthinkable'.[9] Moses, the liberator of the Israelites, who gave them their religion and laws, Freud speculated, was an Egyptian who had formerly been an aide to Akhenaten. Freud reasoned that upon Akhenaten's death the old priesthood at Thebes, which he had suppressed, vented their fury on his memory. The Aten religion was proscribed and Akhenaten's capital city was levelled. The pharaoh and his reforms then became nothing more than a minor incident in Egyptian history, doomed to be forgotten. Freud gave full rein to his imagination. He claimed to believe Moses had looked to Akhenaten for inspiration and leadership. In disappointment and loneliness at the turn of events, Moses addressed himself to the strangers (the Israelites) dwelling in Egypt and sought in them a replacement for what he had lost when Akhenaten died and his religious philosophy was mercilessly crushed.[10]

'He [Moses] chose them for his people and tried to realise his own ideals through them,' Freud suggested. He gave them the Aten religion, which the Egyptians had rejected. 'With an astonishing premonition of later scientific knowledge he [Akhenaten] recognised in the energy of the sun's radiation the source of all life on earth and worshipped the sun as the symbol of his God's power. He gloried in his joy in the Creation and in his life in Maat [truth and harmony]. It is the first case in the history of mankind, and perhaps the purest, of a monotheistic religion'.[11]

Freud therefore maintained that the Exodus had occurred during the Eighteenth Dynasty – Tutankhamun's time – and not the Nineteenth Dynasty as claimed in the Old Testament. These were dangerous times to be thinking such things. He and others of this school of thought such as James Breasted, who taught Hebrew in university classes and had among his students many future rabbis, were alarmed at putting their thoughts to paper in the 1930s, as Hitler rose to power in Germany preaching hatred of the Jews.[12]

'In a world in which anti-Semitic prejudice is still regrettably evident, it seems appropriate to state that the book was not written with the slightest anti-Semitic bias,' Breasted wrote about Freud's final work. 'On the contrary, the author's admiration of Hebrew literature, which began in his boyhood, has always been such that his judgement of it was much more likely to be affected by a favourable bias than otherwise.'[15]

Freud made the connection between Moses and the Egyptian pharaoh. I would now like to take the hypothesis one stage further. The biblical scholar, Ahmed Osman, was the first person to suggest that Akhenaten and Moses were the same man. Through my years of intensive research I have become convinced that he is right; I believe that the papyri in the tomb of Tutankhamun confirmed that Akhenaten, Tutankhamun's father, was Moses, that the visionary pharaoh and great prophet and lawgiver of the Old Testament were one and the same.

Carter's outburst in front of the Vice Consul in Cairo forced me to re-evaluate the biblical account of the Exodus and the links between major biblical figures and the pharaohs. This led me to decide what must have been encrypted in the missing scrolls: that the powerful priests of Amun counter-attacked against the religious revolution started by the visionary Akhenaten, who believed in the one indivisible God without form or substance, and forced the king to abdicate in favour of his son, Tutankhamun, who was only nine years old. This young boy, who had been brought up in the new Atenist religion, was the biblical Christ, the Messiah whose murder and burial were prophesied by Isaiah in the Old Testament.

The young king who Carter discovered encased in gold was not the insignificant pharaoh of history but in actuality the greatest king who ever lived. He built on his father's teachings of the one indivisible God and expanded them to encompass salvation for all. He moulded the pantheon of Egyptian gods into the angels and saints of a later religion.

All trace of the Amarna kings disappeared from the records for thousands of years but, despite efforts to disguise the truth, memories of the events and of the people involved survived in the bloodline of the Messiah. The 'crimson thread' which flowed through the House of David was, in effect, the bloodline of the Egyptian Eighteenth Dynasty.[14]

No wonder the scrolls had to be suppressed. What would have been the repercussions in Israel if the truth had come out that the great Jewish biblical figures were actually pharaohs? That Moses had been kicked out of Egypt rather than heroically leading his people. Equally, would Hitler and the other anti-Semites have been able to continue their campaign of hatred against the Jews, a people who could be proved to have descended from the greatest civilization ever discovered, a civilization of blond, blue-eyed people?

The other question mark which hangs over the disappearance of the scrolls is the role that Carnarvon played. At first he was happy to write to his friend Wallis Budge to say they had found writings which would 'change the thinking of the world'. Then suddenly he was silent on the matter, until his urge for greater wealth and glory got the better of him and he started talking to Samuel Goldwyn in Hollywood. Is it possible that he was persuaded to think better of publicizing the find by his in-laws, the Rothschilds? These were people who were instrumental in the setting up of the state of Israel and by far the most powerful Jewish family in the world. It is equally possible, of course, that this role was performed by the British government, or possibly by the Rothschilds and the government working together.

When you go to the Valley of the Kings, the 'knowledgeable ones' of the tourists will tell you not to bother going into Tutankhamun's tomb, because there is nothing to see except a single mummy. But they do not realize that they are referring to the mortal remains of the Son of God.

Moses, Scrolls and the Murder of Sigmund Freud

Since excavations at Tell el-Amarna by Sir William Flinders Petrie at the end of the nineteenth century, Akhenaten and the Amarna kings have been a source of speculation and fascination to archaeologists and historians. Who were they? What was this strange new religion? What happened to Akhenaten? In his groundbreaking book, *Moses, Pharaoh of Egypt,* Ahmed Osman equates him with the biblical patriarch. For, as surely as Akhenaten is a figure in history, no trace has ever been found of the historical existence of Moses. I first read a copy of Osman's earlier book *Stranger in the Valley of the Kings* ten years ago, in which he postulated that Yuya, interred in the Valley of the Kings, was none other than Joseph, the Jewish patriarch.

I felt as I read that this man really knew how these obscure biblical figures related to the pharaohs of Egypt and I determined to make contact with him. Eventually I reached him by telephone and arranged to meet for lunch at my club. I had never seen even a photograph of him and when he appeared in the dining room he was as much of a stranger to me as Yuya himself. The table was set, there were other diners in the room and after greeting him I came straight to the point, unable to contain myself.

'Before you sit down,' I said, 'I have one question to ask you. I believe that Akhenaten led the Jews out of Egypt.'

'You mean Semites,' he corrected gently.

'Yes,' I said, hardly daring to breathe for fear I would miss his answer.

'Moses led the Semites out of Egypt,' he replied.

'I know,' I said, my heart sinking. 'And I'm wrong.'

Then came one of the most wondrous statements I have ever heard. Looking at me very kindly, he said in a soft voice, 'No, you're not wrong.'

My shout of excitement startled the other diners from their murmured conversations. 'They're the same! They're the same!'

'Yes, they are,' he replied.

I leaned across to him, brushing the cutlery aside and hugged him, a complete stranger, and our friendship began.

I believe that Tutankhamun, who was brought up in the new Atenist movement, was the historical Christ of the Bible, the first in a line of Messiah figures whose tragic murder was prophesied in the Old Testament. He built on his father's teachings of the one indivisible God and expanded them to encompass salvation for all. All traces of the Amarna kings disappeared from the records for thousands of years, but despite efforts to disguise the truth, memories of the events and of the people involved survived. The importance of the missing papyri for the major monotheistic religions of the West could be as great as that of the Dead Sea Scrolls, for they may contain information that will explode old versions of history and ask us to examine our political and religious beliefs in a new light.

15

THE CARTER/
CARNARVON LEGACY

After all my investigations I felt that I was confident enough to commit my suspicions to a book. Others more knowledgeable than myself had heard everything I had to say and they had checked out my theories. There had been no dissent. I knew that it would take a lot more time and work in the valley before I could definitely prove my case once and for all, but I now had more than enough to voice my views on what I am certain happened.

Whatever those missing papyri may have contained, one thing is certain: Howard Carter and Lord Carnarvon were not the heroes that history would have us believe; they were little better than common grave robbers, albeit phenomenally successful ones. In a period when great adventures were still possible, and when the ruling classes of Europe and America were still at liberty to exploit the resources of the rest of the world and call it patronage, the West systematically stripped Egypt of as much of its ancient heritage as possible. We will never know exactly how much Carter and Carnarvon got away with or where it all ended up, but we can be sure that there have been few crimes committed in history which have resulted in such spectacular rewards. They had the contacts – at least Carnarvon did – and the expertise – at least Carter did – and they had the resources (Carnarvon again) necessary for any great business or criminal endeavour. Because Carnarvon was such an integral part of the British establishment, he was able to give their activities the necessary veneer of respectability but, more important than that, they were both able to involve others in their plans – pillars of the establishment such as the great museums – which ensured that there were plenty of influential people with vested interests in not drawing attention to the weaknesses of their story. Once museums and private collectors were implicated in the various deals and agreements, they had as much at stake as the two men themselves. A cloak of secrecy descended over the whole event and although a number of people, such as Thomas Hoving, hinted that things might not be all they should be, the official story still held fast.

By filtering all the news through *The Times*, Carter and Carnarvon gave the most authoritative journalistic voice in the world at the time a vested interest in the project. If other newspapers raised doubts, their complaints could be dismissed as simple professional jealousy. Anything that appeared in *The Times* would be generally considered by the public to be true; cynicism about the press was not as widespread then as it is today. In the end it was just too good a story for anyone to want to destroy. This protection of the story continued because more and more vested interests became involved. When the Tutankhamun exhibition toured the world in the 1970s, a sophisticated marketing machine drew record-breaking crowds in every city as a new generation listened to the tale and marvelled at the sights, ignoring petty academic arguments over exactly whose coffin they were looking at. It didn't matter to them whether it was Tutankhamun's face staring out at them from the billboards or Smenkhkara's; the effect was the same. They didn't care exactly which rooms in which tombs held which relics; it was a beautiful show of colossal wealth, telling of kings of unrivalled power and mystery. No one was interested in the sordid background to the Tutankhamun discovery. It had happened and it was glorious, and that was what was important.

Regardless of whether my theories about the murders are true, or whether there is any substance in the rumours about a mummy's curse, Carnarvon at least did not live long enough to enjoy the fruits of his skulduggery, although the coffers of his family clearly benefited. Carter seemed to gain little pleasure from the material rewards of his crime, but he did manage to secure a place in history for himself, even if he never managed to gain a knighthood or be accepted by the establishment. Lee Keedick, who organized Carter's lecture tour in America, painted a picture of a man who was not at peace with himself at the end.

He was never enjoying himself unless he was in an argument, even over the most insignificant matter, and children could not escape him. Cab drivers, hotel doormen, railroad conductors, Pullman dining car conductors and little flower girls all came in for his invective and acrimonious and irritating comment. He criticized the taxi drivers for their abrupt stops; the hotel porters and doormen for their lack of training. The locomotive engineers did not pass unnoticed. On a long journey he would usually go forward at the first junction stop to the engine and ask the Engineer who taught him to run it, saying he was getting the worst ride of his life by the inept way the train was controlled. All of this infuriated the Engineer and added to the day's turmoil. Once, on a trip from Montreal to Ottawa, he noticed that the Canadian dining car menu requested comments whether or not the food and service were adequate. The menu was an exceptionally large one, and Carter proceeded to write all over the card on both sides the most exasperating and juvenile protestations over the lack of experience of the Company in pretending to operate a dining car, when neither by nature nor training were they prepared for the job. He took keen delight in neatly folding the card and personally mailing it to the Superintendent of the Dining Car Service at Headquarters.[1]

Whether or not it brought happiness to its perpetrators, the Tutankhamun hoax was a spectacular feat of planning and execution. I doubt if such a crime will ever be possible again. It depended for its success on the Egyptian authorities believing they needed people like Carter and Carnarvon. Fortunately, such automatic respect for educated 'gentlemen' no longer exists.

Today, hopefully, it would be impossible for anyone to work in such secrecy for so many years. If journalists didn't find them, television crews would. To pull off a deception of this proportion today you would probably have to be an expert in information technology or the world of international finance. Carter and Carnarvon may have been the last, and greatest, in that long tradition of gentlemen rogues.

Whatever else they achieved, they undoubtedly created one of the greatest tales of all time.

Notes

1 The Greatest Treasure Hunt on Earth

1 Reeves and Taylor, *Howard Carter Before Tutankhamun*, British Museum Press, 1992, p. 188.

2 Hoving, *Tutankhamun: The Untold Story*, New York, 1978.

3 Romer, *The Rape of Tutankhamun*, Michael O'Mara Books, 1993, p. 9.

4 Homer, *The Iliad*, tr. by Alexander Pope, Oxford University Press, 1954.

5 Evans, *Kingdom of the Ark*, Simon and Schuster, 2000, p. 33.

6 Ibid.

7 Reeves and Wilkinson, *The Complete Valley of the Kings*, 1996, pp. 56–7.

8 Ibid.

9 McCoan, *Egypt As It Is*, 1877.

10 Reeves and Wilkinson, *op. cit.*

11 Cotterill, *The Lost Pharaohs*, Hodder and Stoughton, 1975.

12 Edwards, *A Thousand Miles Up the Nile*, London, 1877.

13 Petrie, *Seventy Years of Archaeology*, London, 1933.

14 Ibid.

15 Ibid.

Notes

2 The Significance of Tutankhamun

1 Carter and Mace, *The Tomb of Tut-Ankh-Amen*, 3 vols, London, 1923–33, p. 20.

2 Hoving, *Tutankhamun: The Untold Story*, New York, 1978, p. 17.

3 Elliot Smith, *The Royal Mummies*, CCG, Cairo, 1912.

4 Ibid.

5 Reeves, *The Complete Tutankhamun*, Thames and Hudson, 1990, p. 22.

6 Osman, *The House of the Messiah*, HarperCollins, 1992.

7 Desroches, *Life and Death of a Pharaoh: Tutankhamun*, Penguin Books, 1963, pp. 164–5.

8 Evans, *Kingdom of the Ark*, Simon and Schuster, 2000, p. 118.

9 Ibid.

10 Reeves, *op. cit.*, p. 34.

11 Ibid.

12 Ibid.

3 Howard Carter – Less than a Gentleman

1 James, *Howard Carter: The Path to Tutankhamun*, Kegan Paul Ltd, 1992, pp. 31–45.

2 Frayling, *The Face of Tutankhamun*, Faber and Faber, 1992, p. 68.

3 Reeves, *The Complete Tutankhamun*, Thames and Hudson, 1990, p. 42.

4 James, *op. cit.*

5 Ibid.

6 Reeves and Taylor, *Howard Carter Before Tutankhamun*, British Museum Press, 1992, pp. 23–4.

7 Winstone, *Howard Carter and the Discovery of the Tomb of Tutankhamun*, Constable, 1991, p. 48.

8 Reeves and Wilkinson, *The Complete Valley of the Kings*, Thames and Hudson, 1990, pp. 194–5.

9 Ibid.

10 Ibid.

11 Reeves and Taylor, *op. cit.*

12 James, *op. cit.*

13 Reeves and Wilkinson, *op. cit.*, pp. 70–80.

14 Ibid.

15 Winstone, *op. cit.*, p. 86.

16 Hoving, *Tutankhamun: The Untold Story*, New York, 1978, p. 28.

17 Winstone, *op. cit.*, p. 95.

18 Breasted, *Pioneer to the Past*, London, 1948, p. 155.

19 Reeves and Wilkinson, *op. cit.*

20 Ibid.

4 The Earl of Carnarvon – 'Lordy' of all he Surveys

1 Smith, *Tombs, Temples and Ancient Art*, Norman 1975, p. 80.

2 Hoving, *Tutankhamun: The Untold Story*, New York, 1978, pp. 19–22.

3 Ibid.

4 Ibid.

5 Ibid.

6 Ibid.

7 Reeves, *The Complete Tutankhamun*, Thames and Hudson, 1990, pp. 44–7.

8 Winstone, *Howard Carter and the Discovery of the Tomb of Tutankhamun*, Constable, 1991, pp. 104–6.

9 Carnarvon and Carter, *Five Years Exploration at Thebes*, 1912, p. 32.

10 Reeves, *op. cit.*

11 Hoving, *op. cit.*, pp. 50–1.

Notes

12 Reeves, *op. cit.*

13 Ibid.

14 Hoving, *op. cit.*

15 Reeves, *op. cit.*

16 Winstone, *op. cit.*

17 Reeves, *op. cit.*

18 Hoving, *op. cit.*, pp. 40–7.

19 Reeves, *op. cit.*

20 Hoving, *op. cit.*

21 Ibid.

22 Ibid.

23 Hankey, 'Arthur Weigall, The Tutankhamun Connection', *International Review of Ancient Art and Archaeology*, July/August, 1994, p. 24.

24 Ibid.

5 The Official Story of the Discovery

1 Carter and Mace, *The Tomb of Tut-Ankh-Amen*, 3 vols, London 1923–33, pp. 96–8.

2 Winstone, *Howard Carter and the Discovery of the Tomb of Tutankhamun*, Constable, 1991, p. 121.

3 Carter, *The Discovery of the Tomb of Tutankhamun*, New York, 1977, p. 82.

4 Ibid.

5 Reeves, *The Complete Tutankhamun*, Thames and Hudson, 1990, pp. 50–5.

6 Ibid.

7 Frayling, *The Face of Tutankhamun*, Faber and Faber, 1992, pp. 102–6.

8 Carter and Mace, *op. cit.*

9 Frayling, *op. cit.*

10 Ibid.

11 Carter and Mace, *op. cit.*, pp. 102–4.

12 Winstone, *op. cit.*, p. 144.

13 Frayling, *op. cit.*

14 Reeves and Taylor, *Howard Carter Before Tutankhamun*, British Museum Press, 1992, p. 142.

15 Frayling, *op. cit.*

16 Carter and Mace, *op. cit.*

17 Hoving, *Tutankhamun: The Untold Story*, New York, 1978, pp. 90–7.

18 Reeves, *op. cit.*

19 Hoving, *op. cit.*

20 Ibid.

21 James, *Howard Carter: The Path to Tutankhamun*, Kegan Paul Ltd, 1992, p. 227.

22 Hoving, *Tutankhamun: The Untold Story*, New York, 1978, pp. 106–8.

23 Ibid.

24 Ibid., p. 58.

25 Carter, *op. cit.*, p. 107.

26 Reeves, *op. cit.*.

27 Frayling, *op. cit.*, p. 54.

28 Hoving, *op. cit.*

29 Hoving, ibid., pp. 195–8.

30 Ibid.

6 'Tut' Mania

1 Winstone, *Howard Carter and the Discovery of the Tomb of Tutankhamun*, Constable, 1991, p. 25.

2 Hoving, *Tutankhamun: The Untold Story*, New York, 1978, p. 109.

Notes

3 Hoving, op. cit.

4 Carter and Mace, *The Tomb of Tut-Ankh-Amen*, 3 vols, London, 1923–33, chapter 7.

5 Hoving, *op. cit.*, p. 153.

6 Winstone, *op. cit.*, pp. 178–181.

7 Ibid.

8 Frayling, *The Face of Tutankhamun*, Faber and Faber, 1992, p. 28.

9 Ibid, pp. 10–11.

10 James, *Howard Carter: The Path to Tutankhamun*, Kegan Paul Ltd, 1992, p. 239.

11 Ibid.

12 Reeves and Taylor, *Howard Carter Before Tutankhamun*, British Museum Press, 1992, p. 154.

13 Hoving, *op. cit.*, pp. 145–9.

14 Ibid.

15 Ibid.

16 Ibid.

17 Ibid.

7 The Mummy's Curse

1 Carter and Mace, *The Tomb of Tut-Ankh-Amen*, 3 vols, London, 1923–33, p. 159.

2 Gardiner, *My Working Year*, 1963, p. 40.

3 Frayling, *The Face of Tutankhamun*, Faber and Faber, 1992, pp. 43–51.

4 Desroches-Noblecourt, *Life and Death of a Pharaoh: Tutankhamun*, Penguin Books, 1963, p. 27.

5 Frayling, *op. cit.*

6 Spencer, *Death in Ancient Egypt*, Penguin Books, 1982, p. 93.

7 Frayling, *op. cit.*

Notes

8 Hoving, *Tutankhamun: The Untold Story*, New York, 1978, pp. 164–72.

9 Frayling, *op. cit.*

10 Ibid.

11 Ibid.

12 Brier, *The Murder of Tutankhamun*, Weidenfield and Nicolson, 1998, pp. 151–2.

13 Carter and Mace, *op. cit.*

14 Hoving, *op. cit.*

15 James, *Howard Carter: The Path to Tutankhamun*, Kegan Paul Ltd, 1992.

16 White, *The Tomb of Tutankhamun by Howard Carter*, Iris Press, 1970.

17 Ibid.

18 Ibid.

19 Winstone, *Howard Carter and the Discovery of the Tomb of Tutankhamun*, Constable, 1991, p. 189.

20 Frayling, *op. cit.*

21 Ibid.

22 Ibid.

23 Ibid.

24 Ibid.

25 Ibid.

26 Winstone, *op. cit.*, p. 19.

8 The True Story of Discovery and Robbery

1 Reeves and Wilkinson, *The Complete Valley of the Kings*, Thames and Hudson, 1996, p. 178.

2 Carter, *The Discovery of the Tomb of Tutankhamun*, New York, 1977, p. 186.

3 Ibid.

4 Hoving, *Tutankhamun: The Untold Story*, New York, 1978, pp. 326–8.

Notes

5 Ibid, p. 75.

6 Carter, *op. cit.*, p. 203.

7 Carter and Mace, *The Tomb of Tut-Ankh-Amen*, 3 vols, London, 1923–33, pp. 256–75.

8 Hoving, *op. cit.*, chapter 6.

9 Carter and Mace, *op. cit.*

10 Hoving, *op. cit.*, p. 142–7.

11 Brackman, *The Search for the Gold of Tutankhamun*, Robert Hale Ltd, 1978.

12 Hoving, *op. cit.*

13 Brackman, *op. cit.*

14 Hoving, *op. cit.*

15 White, *The Tomb of Tutankhamun by Howard Carter*, Iris Press, 1970.

16 Hoving, *op. cit.*

17 Ibid.

9 The Cover-Up

1 Scott, Walter, *Pibroch of Donuil Dhu*.

2 Hoving, *Tutankhamun: The Untold Story*, New York, 1978, pp. 64–5.

3 Ibid., pp. 123–5.

4 Ibid.

5 Winstone, *Howard Carter and the Discovery of the Tomb of Tutankhamun*, Constable, 1991, p. 169.

6 Hoving, *op. cit.*

7 Winstone, *op. cit.*

8 Reeves, *The Complete Tutankhamun*, Thames and Hudson, 1990, p. 131.

9 Carter, *The Discovery of the Tomb of Tutankhamun*, New York, 1977, p. 234.

10 James, *Howard Carter: The Path to Tutankhamun*, Kegan Paul Ltd, 1992, p. 218.

11 Reeves and Wilkinson, *The Complete Valley of the Kings*, Thames and Hudson, 1996, p. 72.

12 Carter and Mace, *The Tomb of Tut-Ankh-Amen*, 3 vols, London, 1923–33, p. 10.

13 Hoving, *Tutankhamun: The Untold Story*, New York, 1978, p. 120.

14 Reeves, *op. cit.*, p. 58–9.

15 Hoving, *op. cit.*, pp. 178–9.

16 Frayling, *The Face of Tutankhamun*, Faber and Faber, 1992, p. 115.

17 Carter, *op. cit.*, p. 181.

18 Ibid.

19 Hoving, *op. cit.*, pp. 349–57.

20 Carter, *op. cit.*

21 Ibid.

10 Howard Carter's Grand Finale

1 Reeves, *The Complete Tutankhamun*, Thames and Hudson, 1990, p. 106.

2 Hoving, *Tutankhamun: The Untold Story*, New York, 1978, pp. 264–9.

3 Frayling, *The Face of Tutankhamum*, Faber and Faber, 1992, pp. 129–30.

4 Hoving, *op. cit.*

5 Ibid.

6 Carter and Mace, *The Tomb of Tut-Ankh-Amen*, 3 vols, London, 1923–33, pp. 86–92.

7 Hoving, *op. cit.*

8 Hoving, ibid, p. 288.

9 Frayling, *op. cit.*, p. 31.

10 James, *Howard Carter: The Path To Tutankhamun*, Kegan Paul Ltd, 1992, p. 153.

11 Hoving, *op. cit.*, pp. 318–42.

12 Ibid.

13 Ibid.

14 Ibid.

15 Ibid.

16 Ibid.

17 Ibid.

18 Carter, *The Discovery of the Tomb of Tutankhamun*, New York, 1977.

19 Ibid.

20 Ibid.

21 Ibid.

22 Phillips, *Act of God*, Sidgwick and Jackson, 1998.

23 Hoving, *op. cit.*, pp. 360-1.

24 Ibid.

25 Ibid.

26 Carter and Mace, *op. cit.*, p. 23.

27 Harrison, 'The Tutankhamun Post-Mortem', *Lancet*, 1973.

28 Ibid.

29 Forbes, 'Abusing Pharaoh', *KMT*, Spring 1992.

30 Ibid.

31 Ibid.

32 Carter and Mace, *op. cit.*, p. 345.

33 Hoving, *op. cit.*

34 Reeves and Taylor, *Howard Carter Before Tutankhamun*, British Museum Press, 1992, pp. 178-80.

35 Ibid.

11 The Missing Papyri

1 Hoving, *Tutankhamun: The Untold Story*, New York, 1978, p. 311.

2 Carter, *The Discovery of the Tomb of Tutankhamun*, New York, 1977, p. 197.

3 Hoving, *op. cit.*, pp. 172–5.

4 Ibid.

5 Brackman, *The Search For the Gold of Tutankhamun*, Robert Hale Ltd, 1978.

6 Hoving, *op. cit.*

7 Ibid.

8 Ibid.

9 Carter and Mace, *The Tomb of Tut-Ankh-Amen*, 3 vols, London, 1923–33.

10 Osman, *Moses Pharaoh of Egypt*, Grafton Books, 1990, p. 159.

11 Osman, *Stranger in the Valley of the Kings*, Souvenir Press, 1987.

12 Ibid.

13 Osman, *The House of the Messiah*, Harper Collins, 1992, pp. 165–8.

14 Ibid.

15 Frayling, *The Face of Tutankhamun*, Faber and Faber, 1992, pp. 25–6.

16 Ibid.

17 Breasted, *Pioneer of the Past*, London, 1948, p. 347.

18 Hoving, *Tutankhamun: The Untold Story*, New York, 1978, pp. 222–3.

19 Ibid.

12 A String of Necessary Murders

1 Faulkner, *Book of the Dead*, British Museum Press, 1985, p. 185.

2 White, *The Tomb of Tutankhamun by Howard Carter*, Iris Press, 1970.

3 Ibid.

4 Ibid.

5 Reeves, *The Complete Tutankhamun*, Thames and Hudson, 1990, p. 47.

6 Ibid.

7 Brackman, *The Search for the Gold of Tutankhamun*, Robert Hale Ltd, 1978, p. 184.

8 Ibid.

9 Reeves, *The Complete Tutankhamun*, Thames and Hudson, 1990, p. 63.

10 Brackman, *op. cit.*

11 Weigall, *Tutankhamun and Other Essays*, New York, 1924, pp. 119–36.

12 Ibid.

13 Reeves, *op. cit.*

13 Did Davis, Ayrton and Jones also know too much?

1 Reeves and Wilkinson, *The Complete Valley of the Kings*, Thames and Hudson, 1996, pp. 73–80.

2 Ibid.

3 Smith, *Tombs, Temples and Ancient Art*, Norman, 1956, p. 105.

4 Hoving, *Tutankhamun: The Untold Story*, New York, 1978, p. 118.

5 Reeves and Wilkinson, *op. cit.*

6 Ibid.

7 Aldred, *Akhenaten, King of Egypt*, Thames and Hudson, 1988, pp. 195–219.

8 Ibid.

9 Ibid.

10 Harrison, *An Anatomical Examination of the Pharaonic Remains Purported to be Akhenaten*, JEA 52, 1966.

11 Evans, *Kingdom of the Ark*, Simon and Schuster, 2000, pp. 152–3.

12 Phillips, *Act of God*, Sidgwick and Jackson, 1998.

13 Brackman, *The Search for the Gold of Tutankhamun*, Robert Hale Ltd, 1978, pp. 180–1.

14 Reeves and Wilkinson, *op. cit.*

15 Ibid.

16 White, *The Tomb of Tutankhamun by Howard Carter*, Iris Press, 1970.

17 Weigall, *The Life and Times of Akhenaten, Pharaoh of Egypt*, London, 1923, pp. 283–4.

18 Evans *op. cit.*

19 Aldred, *op. cit.*

20 Reeves, *The Complete Tutankhamun*, Thames and Hudson, 1990, p. 36.

14 Moses, Scrolls and the Murder of Sigmund Freud

1 Freud, *Moses and Monotheism*, Knopf, New York, 1939.

2 Gay, *Freud: A Life for our Time*, Vintage, 1989, pp. 28–52.

3 Freud, *op. cit.*

4 Gay, *op. cit.*

5 Ibid.

6 Ibid.

7 Ibid.

8 Ibid.

9 Freud, *op. cit.*

10 Brackman, *The Search for the Gold of Tutankhamun*, Robert Hale Ltd, London, 1978, pp. 154–5.

11 Ibid.

12 Osman, Ahmed, *Moses: Pharaoh of Egypt*, Grafton Books, London, 1990.

13 Breasted, *History of Egypt*, New York, 1910.

14 Osman, *Stranger in the Valley of the Kings*, Paladin Press, 1989, p. 49.

15 The Carter/Carnarvon Legacy

1 Hoving, *Tutankhamun: The Untold Story*, New York, 1978, pp. 330–1.

BIBLIOGRAPHY

Adams, B., *Egyptian Mummies*, Shire Publications, Princes Risborough, 1984.

Aldred, C., *Akhenaten and Nefertiti*, Thames and Hudson, London, 1973.

– *Akhenaten, King of Egypt*, Thames and Hudson, London, 1988.

– *Jewels of the Pharaohs*, Thames and Hudson, London, 1971.

Alford, A. E., *Gods of the New Millennium*, Hodder and Stoughton, London, 1996.

Allen, T. G., *Discoveries at the Tomb of Tutankhamun*, London, 1924.

Andrea, G., *Egypt in the Age of the Pyramids*, John Murray, London, 1997.

Baigent, M. and Leigh, R., *The Holy Blood and the Holy Grail*, Jonathan Cape, London, 1982.

– *The Dead Sea Scrolls Deception*, Jonathan Cape, London, 1991.

Baikie, J., *Egyptian Antiquities in the Valley*, Methuen, London, 1932.

Baines, J. and Malek, J., *Atlas of Ancient Egypt*, Phaidon, Oxford, 1980.

Barrett, C., *The Egyptian Gods and Goddesses*, London, 1991.

Blackman, A. M., *Luxor and its Temples*, Black, London, 1923.

Brackman, A. C., *The Search for the Gold of Tutankhamun*, Mason/Charter, London, 1976.

Breasted, J. H., *Ancient Records of Egypt*, University of Chicago Press, Chicago, 1906.

– *Pioneer of the Past*, London, 1948.

Brennan, H., *The Atlantis Enigma*, Piatkus, London, 1999.

Bibliography

Brier, B. *The Murder of Tutankhamun*, Weidenfeld and Nicholson, 1998.

Bristowe, S., *The Man Who Built the Great Pyramid*, Williams and Norgate Ltd., London, 1932.

British Library, *Treasures of Tutankhamun*, British Library, London, 1972.

Budge, E. A. W., *The Egyptian Book of the Dead*, New York, 1967.

Butler, Dr. A. J., *The Arab Conquest of Egypt*, University of Oxford, London, 1902.

Carnarvon and Carter, *Five Years Exploration at Thebes*, London, 1912.

Carter, H., *The Tomb of Tutankhamun*, Sphere Books Ltd., London, 1972.

– *Tut. Ankh. Amun. The Politics of Discovery*, Libri Publications, London, 1998.

– and Mace, A. C., *The Tomb of Tut-Ankh-Amen*, 3 vols, Cassell and Company Ltd., 1923–33.

– *The Discovery of the Tomb of Tutankhamun*, Dover Publications Inc., New York, 1977.

Cayce, E., *The Egyptian Heritage*, Edgar Cayce Foundation, 1984.

Ceram, C. W., *The World of Archaeology*, Thames and Hudson, London, 1966.

Cheik, A. D., *The African Origin of Civilization*, Chicago, 1955.

Clayton, P. A., *Chronicles of the Pharaohs*, Thames and Hudson, London, 1984.

Cohen, D., *Ancient Egypt*, Doubleday, New York, 1990.

Cotterell, M., *The Tutankhamun Prophecies*, Headline Books, London, 1999.

Cottrell, L., *Digs and Diggers*, Butterworth Press, London, 1966.

– *The Secrets of Tutankhamun*, Lawrence Hill Books, London, 1978.

– *The Lost Pharaohs*, Hodder and Stoughton, London, 1975.

David, R. and David, A. E., *A Biographical Dictionary of Ancient Egypt*.

Dawson, W. and Uphill, E., *Who Was Who in Egyptology*, Egyptian Expl. Society, London, 1925.

Bibliography

Desroches, Noblecourt C., *Life and Death of a Pharaoh: Tutankhamun*, Penguin Books, London, 1963.

Drosnink, M., *The Bible Code*, Orion Publishing, London, 1997.

Dunstan, Victor, *Did the Virgin Mary Live and Die in England?*, Megiddo Press, Wales, 1985.

Durant, W. and M., *Our Oriental Heritage*, New York, 1963.

Eaton-Krauss, M., *The Tomb of Tutankhamun*, British Library Catalogue, London, 1993.

Edwards, A, *A Thousand Miles Up The Nile*, London, 1877.

Eisenman, R. and Wise, M., *The Dead Sea Scrolls Uncovered*, Element, Dorset, 1996.

Evans, L, *Kingdom of the Ark*, Simon and Schuster, 2000.

Fagin, *The Rape of the Nile*

Flinders-Petrie, W. M., *The Early Dynastic Cemeteries* (with chapters by A. C. Mace), Egyptological Exp. Fund, London, 1898–9.

Fox, P., *Tutankhamun's Treasury*, London, 1951.

Frayling, C., *The Face of Tutankhamun*, Faber and Faber, 1992.

Frazier, Sir J., *The Golden Bough: Studies in the History of Oriental Religion, Adonis, Attis and Osiris*, Macmillan and Co. Ltd., London, 1922.

Freud, S., *Sigmund Freud and Art, His Personal Collection* (Introduction by Peter Gay), Thames and Hudson Ltd., London, 1989.

Freud, S., *Moses and Monotheism*, Knopf, New York, 1939.

Ferguson, N., *The World's Banker: The History of the House of Rothschild*, London, 1988.

Gardiner, A., *My Working Year*, London, 1923.

Gardner, L., *Genesis of the Grail Kings*, Bantam Press, London, 1988.

– *Bloodline of the Holy Grail*, Bantam Press, London, 1995.

Bibliography

Gay, P., *Freud: A Life for our Times*, J. M. Dent, London, 1998.

Gilbert, A. and Cotterell, M., *The Mayan Prophecies*, Element Books, London, 1995.

Graves, R., *The White Goddess*, Faber Ltd., London, 1961.

Grimal, N., *A History of Ancient Egypt*, USA, 1992.

Harnes, J. E. and Wente, F. F., *X-Ray Atlas of the Royal Mummies*, USA, 1980.

Herodotus, *The Histories*, Penguin Press, London, 1954.

Hooker, J. T., *Reading the Past*, Guild Publishing, London, 1980.

Hornung, E., *The Valley of the Kings*, New York, 1990.

Hoving, T., *Tutankhamun: The Untold Story*, New York, 1978.

James, T. G. H., *Ancient Egypt*, British Museum Publishing, London, 1988.

- *Howard Carter: The Path To Tutankhamun*, Kegan Paul Ltd, 1992.

Joukowsky, M., *Field Archaeology*, New York, 1967.

Jung, C. G., *Memories, Dreams and Reflections*, Collins and Routledge, London, 1963.

Kastner, J., *The Wisdom of Ancient Egypt*, USA, 1967.

Knight, C. and Lomas, R., *The Hiram Key*, Century, London, 1996.

Kramer, S. N., *Cradle of Civilization*, Time Life Books, USA, 1967.

Kyriakos, M., *Copts and Moslems Under British Control*, Smith Elder and Co., London, 1911.

Laidler, K., *The Head of God*, Weidenfeld and Nicolson, London, 1998.

Landay, J. M., *The House of David*, Weidenfeld and Nicolson, London, 1973.

Lefkowitz, M. and Rogers, G., *Black Athena Revisited*, University of North Carolina Press, c 1996.

Lockhart, D., *Jesus the Heretic*, Element Books, London, 1997.

Bibliography

Lucas, A., *Ancient Egyptian Materials and Industries: Histories and Mysteries of Man*, Edward Arnold, London, 1926; 4th edn ed. J. R. Harris, Edward Arnold, London, 1962.

Mace and Winlock, *The Tomb of Senebtisi at Lisht*, Metropolitan Museum, New York, 1916.

Mace, A. C., *The Early Dynastic Cemeteries at Naga-ed-Der: Part II*, Metropolitan Museum, Germany, 1909.

– *Work at the Tomb of Tutankhamun*, Egyptian Expl. Society, London and New York, 1922.

Mack, Burton, L., *The Lost Gospel: The Book of Q and Christian Origins*, Harper, USA, 1993.

Manniche, L., *City of the Dead: Thebes in Egypt Horizon of Eternity*, British Museum Press, London, 1978.

McCoan, *Egypt As It Is*, London, 1877.

Moorehead, A., *The White Nile*, New York, 1960.

Murray, M. A., *The Splendour that was Egypt*, Book Club Association, London, 1997.

Naville, E., *The Temple of Deir El Bahari*, London, 1895.

Noone, R. W., *Ice: The Ultimate Disaster*, Harmony Books, New York, 1994.

Nott, S. C., *Teachings of Gurdjieff*, Routledge and Kegan Paul, London, 1974.

Oliphant, M., *The Atlas of the Ancient World*, USA, 1992.

– *The Encyclopedia of Ancient Egypt*, USA, 1991.

– *Stranger in the Valley of the Kings*, Souvenir Press, USA, 1987.

– *Moses, Pharaoh of Egypt*, Grafton Books, London, 1990.

Osman, A., *The House of the Messiah*, HarperCollins, London, 1992.

– *Out of Egypt*, Century, London, 1998.

Bibliography

Palels, E., *The Gnostic Gospels*, Vintage Books, USA, 1998.

Partridge, R., *Transport in Ancient Egypt*, London, 1996.

Parva, D., *Cemeteries of Abadiyeh and Hu*, Metropolitan Museum, New York, 1960.

Pauwels, L., *Gurdjieff*, Times Press Ltd., London, 1964.

Peet, T. E. and Wooley, L., *The City of Akhenaton*, London, 1923.

Pendlebury, J. D. S., *Tell El Amarna*, London, 1935.

Perl, L., *Mummies, Tombs and Treasure*, 1997.

Petrie, W. F. *Seventy Years of Archaeology*, London, 1933.

Phillips, G., *Act of God*, Sidgwick and Jackson, London, 1998.

- *Moses, Tutankhamun and the Myth of Atlantis*, Sidgwick and Jackson, London, 1998.

Redford, D. B., *Akhenaton: The Heretic King*, New York, 1984.

Reeves, C. N., *Into the Mummy's Tomb*, Time Quest Books, London, 1996.

- *The Complete Tutankhamun*, Thames and Hudson, London, 1990.

Reeves, C. N., Keegan, P., *The Valley of the Kings*, London, 1990.

Reeves, C. N. and Taylor, J., *Howard Carter Before Tutankhamun*, British Museum Press, 1992.

Reeves C. N. and Wilkinson, *The Complete Valley of the Kings*, Thames and Hudson, 1996.

Rice, M., *Egypt's Making*, Routledge, London, 1990.

Rogers, G., *Quo Vadis?*

Romer, J., *Valley of the Kings*, London, 1981.

- *The Tomb of Tutankhamun*, London, 1983.

Romer, J. and R., *The Rape of Tutankhamun*, Michael O'Mara Books, London, 1993.

Romer, J. and E., *The Seven Wonders of the World*, Michael O'Mara Books, London, 1995.

Bibliography

Salibi, K., *The Bible Came from Arabia: A Radical Reinterpretation of Old Testament Geography*, Pan Books, London, 1985.

- *Conspiracy in Jerusalem: The Hidden Origins of Jesus*, I. B. Tauris and Co. Ltd, London, 1988.

Schonfield, H. J., *Those Incredible Christians: A New Look at the Early Church*, Hutchinson, London, 1968.

- *The Essene Odyssey*, Element Books, London, 1984.

- *The Passover Plot*, Element Books, London, 1985.

Sitchin, Z., *The Twelfth Planet*, Element Books, New York, 1977.

- *The Stairway to Heaven*, Element Books, New York.

- *The Wars of Gods and Man*, Element Books, New York.

- *The Lost Realms*, Element Books, New York.

- *Genesis Revisited*, Element Books, New York, 1990.

Smith, G. E., *The Royal Mummies*, Cairo, 1912.

Smith, J. L, *Tombs, Temples and Ancient Art*, Norman, 1975.

Spencer, A. J., *Death in Ancient Egypt*, London, 1982.

- *Early Egypt: The Rise of Civilization*, London, 1993.

Thiering, B., *Jesus the Man*, Transworld, London, 1992.

Time Life London, *What Life Was Like on the Banks of the Nile*, Time Life, London, 1998.

Time/Life, *Egypt, Land of the Pharaohs*, Time/Life, USA 1992.

Times Books, *The Times Concise Atlas of the Bible*, Times Books, London, 1991.

Tyldesley, J., *Hatshepsut: The Female Pharaoh*, Penguin Books, London, 1996.

Van Broek and G. Quisbel, *Corpus Hermeticum*, In de Pelikaan, Amsterdam, 1996.

Bibliography

Vanderberg, P., *The Curse of the Pharaohs*, J. B. Lippincott and Co., USA, 1975.

Velikovsky, I., *Ages in Chaos*, Sidgwick and Jackson, London, 1952.

– *Oedipus and Akhenaten*, Doubleday, New York, 1960.

– *Worlds in Collision*, Victor Gollancz, London, 1973.

Verner, M., *Forgotten Pharaohs: Lost Pyramids – 'Abusir'*, Czech Institute of Egyptology, Prague, 1994.

Weigall, A., *Archaeology in the Open*.

– *A Guide to the Antiquities of Upper Egypt*, Methuen and Co., London, 1910.

– *The Treasury of Ancient Egypt*, Wm. Blackwood and Sons, London, 1911.

– *The Glory of the Pharaohs*, Thornton Butterworth, London, 1923.

– *Life and Times of Akhenaten*, Blackwoods, London, 1923.

– *Tutankhamun and Other Essays*, Butterworth, London, 1923.

– *History of the Pharaohs II*, Thornton Butterworth, London, 1927.

– *A Short History of Ancient Egypt*, Chapman and Hull, London, 1934.

Welsh, F., *Tutankhamun's Egypt*, Shire Egyptology, London, 1993.

White, J. M., *Carter*, London.

– *The Tomb of Tutankhamun by Howard Carter*, Iris Press, 1970.

Wilkinson, J. G., *The Manners and Customs of Ancient Egptians* (3 Volumes), London, 1988.

Wilson, C., *From Atlantis to the Sphinx*, London, 1986.

Wilson, J. A., *Signs And Wonders Upon Pharaoh*, London, 1964.

Winston, H. V. F., *Howard Carter and the Discovery of the Tomb of Tutankhamun*, Constable, 1991.

INDEX

Index

Index

Index

Index